# THE

# BAD OLD DAYS

A Decade of Struggling for Justice in Louisiana

HERBERT ROTHSCHILD JR.

Fulton Books, Inc.
Meadville, PA

Published by Fulton Books 2021

ISBN 978-1-63710-904-5 (paperback)
ISBN 978-1-63710-906-9 (hardcover)
ISBN 978-1-63710-905-2 (digital)

Printed in the United States of America

For the women and men who've worked for the ACLU, both volunteers and staff, the unsung defenders of American freedom.

# Preface

Prior to the thirty-fifth reunion in New Orleans of Isidore Newman School's Class of 1957, of which I am a member, one of the organizers sent around a questionnaire. Among other questions, it asked how the sixties had affected us. The class was small—fewer than fifty—and the number of responses was smaller, but I was struck by how many reported that the tumultuous events of those times hadn't made much difference to them. Their focus had been on starting careers and families.

It's true that because of our privilege, we could insulate ourselves from the tumult. Private schools and upscale neighborhoods were under no pressure to integrate racially, and it wasn't hard to escape being drafted into combat in Vietnam—there were exemptions, deferments, and enlistments in the National Guards. So if we did engage in those extraordinary upheavals, it was largely a matter of choice. Still, it was hard for me to understand why only a few of us who stayed in Louisiana or returned after completing our higher education were drawn into the action. During the years 1966–1976, which are my primary focus in this book, the South except for some rural pockets was transformed from a closed to an open society, one ruled by law instead of custom. In its most important aspect, the world in which we had grown up vanished. A society that had organized itself around the systematic and total subordination of Black people came to resemble the rest of the country.

Which means that the South didn't rid itself of the curse of racism, but it is no longer totalitarian. Knowing when and where I was raised, my friends in Oregon, where I now reside, occasionally ask me whether the racial situation really has improved. My response is that it's almost impossible to imagine what it was like to live all one's life without protection of the law—that you must stomach constant humiliation, that any perceived sign of "uppityness" might bring the direst consequences, that people can beat and rape and kill you with impunity.

I rarely volunteer such information. Black people don't want a White man saying what can sound to them like "You never had it so good." And I don't want to dissuade anyone from deep engagement in efforts to overcome continuing injustice. But the struggles and sacrifices of those times were not in vain.

It's inevitable that popular understanding of the Civil Rights Movement foregrounds a few leaders and a handful of pivotal events. From the start, MLK was the public face of the Southern Christian Leadership Conference and Stokely Carmichael of the Student Nonviolent Coordinating Committee, whereas it took years for Ella Baker's crucial contributions to both organizations to gain recognition. And Frank Minis Johnson Jr., the extraordinary federal judge for the Middle District of Alabama, of whom Bill Moyers said, he "altered forever the face of the South," was reduced to the equivalent of a footnote in the 2014 film *Selma*. The struggles had to be waged on countless fronts by countless people, few of whom were ever more than locally noted. One of my intentions in this work is to validate that claim and honor some of those people.

The Civil Rights Movement was the primary driver of the change from a closed to an open society. It was the one that stirred my conscience and persuaded me to seek an academic position in the South after I completed my graduate studies at Harvard in 1965.[1] But pressure for change soon emerged on a broad front.

Lyndon Johnson's escalation of the war in Vietnam projected into the public forum large numbers of White people, especially those of draft age on college campuses. Black liberation emboldened other oppressed groups—women, students, gays—to organize and advocate for themselves. And institutional responses to a rapidly changing and assertive youth culture sensitized middle class kids to the arbitrary exercise of authority. The South's social prohibition of public controversy couldn't withstand this multi-faceted onslaught of outspokenness.

As its force waned, the long-standing customary prohibition of dissent allied itself with attempts at legal prohibition. Because most of my work was done through the American Civil Liberties Union, I was involved in almost all those struggles. In some, such as the Civil Rights and Women's movements, my role was supportive. In others, especially First Amendment exercise, the rights of the mentally ill, and the reform of criminal procedure, I was more prominent. My emphases in the following pages aren't based on an objective assessment of the relative importance of various struggles but on my ability to provide a useful amount of firsthand information.

\*\*\*\*\*

I founded the Baton Rouge Chapter of the ACLU of Louisiana in mid-1966 and guided it for its first four years. Most of the early members were associated with LSU, where I was teaching in the English Department. For three years, it was extraordinarily difficult to find cooperating attorneys, those who would take cases *pro bono*, and the state affiliate didn't get a staff attorney until 1971. So we had to rely heavily on public exposure and persuasion. Soon, however, a number of young men and women coming out of the LSU Law School were attracted to such work. I think I was an influence on them, both through personal interactions and having raised the profile of civil liberties. Probably the larger influence, though, was the spirit of the age, the sense that "the times they are a-changing."

Our chapter brought to the ACLU of Louisiana a presence at the state legislature. Because the legislature met in Baton Rouge and the New Orleans-based state ACLU couldn't afford to pay a lobbyist, it hadn't been able to stop the passage of bad bills much less seek passage of good ones. Thanks to our chapter, beginning in 1968, that changed. Some of our most important achievements were legislative.

We also served as a corrective to the insularity of the state organization. Before we formed, the affiliate's work had been confined to New Orleans. I became increasingly prominent in its leadership, serving as state vice-president in 1969 and then president from 1970 to mid-1972, when I moved my family to California for a sabbatical year. As president, forming chapters elsewhere in the state was my main priority. By fall of 1971, seven chapters and 40 percent of the membership were outside New Orleans.

After I returned from California in June 1973, I rejoined the chapter board and also assumed the position of state legislative director. There were still important struggles to be waged, but the work had become easier thanks to the changes wrought primarily by the impact of newly-won Black political power. The most striking testimony to progress was the Declaration of Rights in the Constitution of 1974. Gov. Edwin Edwards had convened a convention the year before to rewrite the one adopted in 1921, an enormously long and cumbrous document that required constant amending at the voting booth. Progressive lawyers—notably Camille Gravel, a close ally of Edwards—dominated the Committee on the Bill of Rights and Elections and welcomed ACLU input. The final product, adopted when voters passed the new constitution, largely brought Louisiana law into consonance with the US Bill of Rights and the federal jurisprudence interpreting it.

The bellwether change, perhaps, was its equal protection clause. The 1921 constitution had no equal protection guarantee. The new constitution prohibited any discrimination on the basis of race or religion. Because those prohibitions were absolute, LSU Law Professor Lee Hargrave, who served as director of the Louisiana Constitutional Convention Records Commission and assistant clerk of the convention, wrote that when it was adopted, the new constitution even went "beyond the decisional law construing the Fourteenth Amendment of the United States Constitution."[2]

*****

Inevitably, the recollections I share are self-revelatory. Still, I consider this work more a grassroots history than a memoir. With the partial exception of the first chapter, in which I explain my relationship to the place where the events I recount occurred, my focus is on me only insofar as I was involved in those events.

Given that I mean to transcend mere personal history, when it seemed appropriate, I have tried to correct the insufficiencies of my memory through research. Besides the online archives of the *Baton Rouge Morning Advocate* and the *States-Times*, I have relied on the archives of the Baton Rouge Chapter of the ACLU and the Baton Rouge Human Relations Council, both housed in the Hill Memorial Library of the Louisiana State University Libraries, and on the archives of the ACLU of Louisiana, housed at the Howard-Tilton Memorial Library of Tulane University. I wish to thank the staff of those institutions for their gracious assistance.

There are many ACLU friends and colleagues who don't get mentioned in the following pages but whose work helped transform Louisiana, some more than mine did. I carry their names with me. Like all of us who have written the ACLU's proud history, they were the undecorated heroes in the continuing struggle to preserve and defend our liberties.

*****

I want to explain why I sometimes put the words *black* and *white* in lower case but mostly in upper case, which is not standard usage. I mean to distinguish in that way reference to color from reference to race. I capitalize references to race because I consider race to be a socially constructed identity with only a loose relationship to skin color.

From the multiple experiences that shaped that understanding of race I choose two. Recounting them will provide a sample of the narratives to come.

My first story. Early in 1967, I learned that Carol Prejean, a Black graduate student at Louisiana State University, had become engaged to marry a White man named John Zippert. John had come down from New York to work with Black farmers in southwest Louisiana, the area of the state where Carol's family lived.[3] At that time interracial marriage was illegal in Louisiana. I referred Carol to the ACLU's state office in New Orleans. Dick Sobol, who was working for Lawyers Constitutional Defense Committee out of that office, agreed to represent her.

As expected, the clerk of court in Lafayette Parish refused to issue the marriage license, so Sobol went to federal court. Earlier in its 1966–1967 term, the US Supreme Court had heard arguments in *Loving v. Virginia*, which challenged the anti-miscegenation statute in that state. So the Louisiana court deferred action until the ruling in *Loving v. Virginia* was announced. On June 12 it was; states could not outlaw racially-mixed marriages. The marriage license was then granted to John and Carol, and they were wed in a Roman Catholic church in Lafayette.

Sobol attended and with delight explained at the next ACLU board meeting what happened. There was a crowd of reporters outside the church. When the newlyweds emerged, the reporters did a double-take. They couldn't tell which one of the couple was White and which was Black.

My second story. In 1970, the Louisiana legislature passed a law defining a Black person as having one-thirty-second "Negro blood." That statute replaced the centuries'-old standard, "any traceable amount" of Negro ancestry, for designating race on official documents like birth certificates. The state ACLU received an appeal for help in challenging the statute. When the matter was discussed at the next state board meeting, one member asked what the criterion should be. My answer was that racial identity shouldn't be legally defined but left to the discretion of each person.

In 1983, the legislature repealed the 1970 law. On that occasion, the State Health Department lawyer who had defended the statute against a legal challenge to it said that as a practical matter the law was "useless" and "impossible" to apply because of the difficulty in precisely determining a person's racial background.[4]

---

[1]  The most decisive moment for me was when James Cheney, Andrew Goodman, and Michael Schwerner were murdered in Neshoba County, Mississippi, in the summer of 1964. I have carried their names with me ever since.

[2]  Lee Hargrave, "The Declaration of Rights of the Louisiana Constitution of 1974," *Louisiana Law Review*, volume 35, number [Fall 1974], p. 6. We tried but failed to persuade the committee to include sex among the absolute prohibitions. The constitution permits discriminations on the basis of sex, as well as "birth, age, culture, physical condition, or political

ideas or affiliations" if such discriminations are not "arbitrary, capricious or unreasonable."

3   I knew Carol because she had come to me seeking to challenge the loyalty oath all LSU employees were then required to sign. Signing it was a condition of her holding a teaching assistantship. I couldn't give her much hope of success because the US Supreme Court had upheld "affirmative" oaths (those that pledge loyalty rather than forswear certain beliefs or associations), and the LSU oath was affirmative. Carol and John later moved to Eutaw, Alabama, to serve farmers in the state's impoverished Black Belt. Carol won distinction as an educator, organizer, newspaper publisher, and poet.

4   The legal challenge had been brought by Susie Guillory Phipps, the wife of a well-to-do White businessman in Sulphur, Louisiana, to change the racial description on her birth certificate from "col." to "white." At the time of repeal, she still hadn't prevailed in her quest. Interestingly, a new law was then passed that required "a preponderance of evidence" for changing the racial designation, replacing the former requirement of evidence that left "no room for doubt." Sworn statements from family members, doctors, and others would suffice.

# Chapter 1

## "I thought you were from New York."

When I was young and heard Southern accents in films set in New Orleans, I'd think with some contempt that the directors should have known better. Later, after life had forced me to put aside the arrogance of my youth, I tumbled to the real explanation: they knew their audiences wouldn't believe New Orleanians speak the way we actually do.

Usually, I can recognize people from my hometown by their accent and vice versa. People from elsewhere cannot. They tend to assume we're from somewhere on the East Coast. In fairness, we do sound as if we're from Brooklyn.

Which brings me to my first meeting with St. John Chilton.

It didn't take long, after I founded the local chapter of the American Civil Liberties Union in 1966, for me to become a public figure. In those days, there weren't many White people in Baton Rouge who openly supported the Civil Rights Movement. So it was that I soon received a letter on White Citizens' Council stationery signed by St. John Chilton. It wasn't threatening, but it was ugly.

The White Citizens' Councils were founded across the deep South immediately after the US Supreme Court declared "separate but equal" unconstitutional in its *Brown v. Board of Education* decision of 1954. Hodding Carter III, in his book on the White Citizens' Councils titled *The South Strikes Back*, called them "the uptown Klan."[1] It's true that the membership tended to be middle class rather than blue collar and country, but some of the South's most virulent segregationists, such as Byron de la Beckwith, who murdered Medgar Evers, belonged to the Councils.[2]

"Who is St. John Chilton?" I asked my colleague Nick Canaday. Nick had come to Louisiana State University about eight years before I arrived and was the only other liberal activist in the English Department at that time. "He's the chairman of the Department of Botany and Plant Pathology," Nick answered, to my surprise. Chilton was rather notorious, Nick went on to say. Among other stories told about him was that he kept a handgun in his office desk. So much for the widespread notion that education is the key to moral advance.

Chilton had done significant work in his academic specialty, the diseases of sugarcane. Louisiana produced a lot of cane, especially in the parishes on the Mississippi upriver from New Orleans. I had grown up with Mike Godchaux, whose family owned a major sugar company bearing their name in St. John the Baptist Parish. Mike was one of the most intelligent people I ever knew—and I've known many. He was also big and strong, so as kids, we always wanted to be on the same team with him when we played games like Capture the Flag and Message to Garcia.

Not long after my conversation with Nick, I came out of my office building at the end of a workday to discover that my bicycle had a flat tire. I walked across campus to a road leading in the direction of my home and stuck out my thumb. In less than a minute, a large tan Cadillac with some years on it stopped for me.

I got into the front passenger seat and thanked the driver. Then I put out my hand and said, "I'm Herb Rothschild."

The driver, who didn't take my hand and whose face was expressionless, replied, "I know who you are. I'm St. John Chilton."

I said to myself, *Oh shit.* I can't remember what I said to Chilton.

Then I heard a voice. It was as clear as if someone were speaking to me. It said, "Tell this man you're from New Orleans."

So I quickly created a pretext to do so. "Oh," he said, "I thought you were from New York." To bolster my *bona fides*, I mentioned my friendship with Mike Godchaux, who, predictably, he had known as well. By this time, his face had relaxed. The remainder of the ten-minute ride was entirely pleasant, and our subsequent meetings on campus were cordial.

In St. John Chilton's mind, I had morphed from Outside Agitator to Local Radical. Every Southern town could tolerate one of those.

*****

My roots in south Louisiana run fairly deep. They run through my mother.

My father was from Columbus, Georgia. He came to New Orleans to take a position at the Tulane Medical School after he finished his residency in pediatrics. When he was ninety, he began to tell the story that then-governor Huey P. Long had asked him in 1931 to join the faculty of the newly opened LSU Medical School, which was Long's cherished creation, as was its associated Charity Hospital, where any Louisiana resident, Black or White, could get free care. Dad said that he turned down Long's offer because he wanted to enter private practice. The first time I heard that story, I asked Mother if Dad had ever told it to her when he was younger. When she said "no," I asked her if she thought it was true. Her reply was, "If it isn't, there's no one still alive who can contradict him."

Actually, Dad did accept Long's offer, only it was more than a half century after one of the few great people Louisiana has ever produced was assassinated. When Dad retired from private practice at the age of eighty-three, having built the Rothschild Pediatric Group into the largest in the state, he taught clinical pediatrics at LSU for the next five years. Annually now, the Herbert Rothschild Award, established by the Greater New Orleans Pediatric Society and the LSU Department of Pediatrics, is given to an outstanding graduating senior in that specialty.

Mother was the South Louisiana native. She lived in New Orleans from her birth in 1912 to her death in 2002, save for two years in New York earning a master's degree in journalism from Columbia University. After spending the first twenty years of her married life in the same pursuits of leisure that almost all her women friends did, she devoted enough of the remainder of her life to civic work to earn distinction apart from being the doctor's wife.

While a number of organizations were fortunate enough to enlist her help, Mother's involvement with two of them led to significant positions and to prominence. One was the New Orleans Symphony. In those days, symphonies, like many other organizations, had "big" boards on which men sat, and parallel women's boards, often called auxiliaries, which had far less decision-making authority but did most of the work. Mother became president of the women's board and for a time was national president of the Association of Major Symphony Orchestra Volunteers. During her tenure, she was interviewed by *The New York Times* and created something of a stir back home by saying that the arts in New Orleans weren't flourishing because members of the city's ruling class spent most of their money on Mardi Gras balls, which are all about their daughters' debuts.

The other organization was the Metropolitan Opera. It has long had a program of systematically searching out talented singers in the provinces and bringing them to New York for further training and to jump-start their careers. For many years, Mother ran the auditions at the district and then the regional level. When the Met celebrated its one hundredth anniversary, she was seated on the stage at Lincoln Center during one of the performances.

In the last two decades of Mother's life, any fledgling arts enterprise in New Orleans sought her help, and not because she gave large sums. Rather, it was that her managerial skills were so highly developed and her name carried such weight. Had she been born fifty years later, I think she would have been the CEO of a major corporation.

Mother's mother was also born in New Orleans. Her parents had moved there from Alsace. Mother's father was born in Plaquemines Parish, which extends on both sides of the Mississippi south of New Orleans down to the Gulf. Its farthest reach is Pilottown, where ocean-going ships must take on a licensed pilot to navigate the powerful, treacherous waters of the river. Papú, as we called him, lived a bit upriver in Bohemia, close to Pointe à la Hache, the county seat. Before Hurricane Katrina, Bohemia had a population of two hundred; after the hurricane, only twenty-five houses were standing.

Papú's family was named Davis, having changed their name from Wolf, which amused me enormously when I learned of it in my young adulthood. When his parents emigrated from Poland, they settled in Plaquemines Parish and took up rice farming. I never knew why. It was an unusual occupation for Jews in the United States. But Papú's rural life ended when, in his teens, the family moved up to New Orleans, as did his first cousins the Haspels, whose family had also been farming down there. After high school, Papú entered a more characteristically Jewish occupation, the wholesale ladies' garment business.

His first cousins also entered the *schmatta*, or "rag" trade, as it's called in Yiddish, only with far more success. In 1909, Joe Haspel struck it rich with the seersucker suit, which became a staple of men's summer wear throughout the South and well beyond. I grew up knowing all the members of the second generation, who were my mother's age. In the third generation, no one wanted to continue the business, and the label was sold to Palm Beach. But it was later bought back by family members, and in its various reincarnations, the Haspel seersucker suit may still be seen walking the streets of New Orleans.

Papú made a decent living in a business destined for obsolescence. For much of his work life, he would travel each year by packet boat to the garment district in New York City, select the clothing he would display at trunk shows in railroad hotel lobbies in small towns around Louisiana, then take a commission on the orders he placed with the Seventh Avenue factories. He had the good sense to retire before there was no more demand for such service.

When he did, Papú bought a twenty-five-foot cabin cruiser and docked it for some ten years in Pointe à la Hache. The marshes down there were among the richest wetland environments in the country, and the fishing, crabbing, and oystering were fine.

All that is still largely true, but Louisiana is losing its coastal wetlands at an alarming rate, thanks largely to the oil companies' service channels, which honeycomb the marshes and let the tidal surges come way up and drag out the grasses. Predictably, they blame the loss on the natural subsidence that is no longer offset by alluvial deposits, since the Mississippi is diked down to its several mouths. There is some, but not enough, truth to this defense. The fossil fuel corporations have had their way down there, and they haven't been forced to take responsibility for the damage they've done.

Papú often took me fishing with him. In the first few years, we'd trawl for our bait, because there was no season on shrimping then. What I liked even better than the fishing was when the trawl net was pulled aboard and its contents spilled onto the deck. The experience was akin to the excitement of opening presents when I was a little boy; you never knew what would be inside. Sometimes it was disappointing—just jellyfish turned shapeless by the handling and a few small crabs. But usually it was an aquatic cornucopia—shrimp, crabs, small fish of various species, an occasional oyster where the net had scraped the bottom. Everything got thrown back except the shrimp, which was the bait we were after. That didn't matter. What counted were the surprises coming out of the deep.

Sometimes, residents of Pointe à la Hache would go out with us. I especially remember Telu Fontenelle, who ran the jail. He was a small and, to me, an odd man, the product of a world quite different from New Orleans, even though fewer than thirty miles away as the crow flies. About my grandfather's age, Telu outlived him and came up to Papú's funeral, where he conversed so loudly in his Cajun accent at the back of the receiving room that my great aunt asked me to shush him.

Some dozen years later, I was briefly chatting with Lee Perez, then district attorney of Plaquemines Parish, in the hall outside a committee room at the Louisiana legislature. I mentioned having known Telu. Lee said that until he was eighty years old, Telu would come up to New Orleans once a week to get laid. It wouldn't have occurred to me that he would set the bar so high for the rest of us.

Lee was Leander Perez Jr. His father, who had recently died, for decades had ruled Plaquemines Parish and the adjacent St. Bernard Parish with an iron hand. His control was both political and economic because he had gotten immensely rich from subleasing state mineral lands and from payoffs by oil companies for illegal deals he brokered between them and the Plaquemines levee boards. In addition to being a crook and a political thug, Leander Sr. was a hardcore, vicious racist and an anti-Semite. He dictated the state's response to court-ordered desegregation of the schools from 1960 into 1964, while Jimmy Davis was governor. The laws he got the legislature to pass did credit to the police state Perez presided over in Plaquemines Parish, such as making it a crime to advocate racial integration and a legal requirement to report anyone who did so.[3]

New Orleans Archbishop Joseph Rummel excommunicated Perez in 1962 for opposing his efforts to integrate the Catholic schools, which included one in St. Bernard Parish that was burned down. In effect, Perez then set up his own church of racists. An older colleague of mine in the English Department said that he had gone down on university business to Buras, where Perez had his office. The person he was dealing with at one point motioned him to come into Perez's office after ascertaining that it was unoccupied. He went up to Perez's desk, genuflected, and made the sign of the cross. He said, only half-jokingly, "I guess you can call me a Perezbyterian."

I was disgusted to realize, when Perez died in 1969 and was given a funeral mass at Holy Name Church in uptown New Orleans, that Rummel's successor, Philip Hannon, had lifted the excommunication without requiring a public recantation.

*****

While part of my White family originated downriver of New Orleans, all of my Black family came from upriver. There are both Black and White folks named Becnel in Reserve, where the Godchaux sugar mill was located. I suspect they are unacknowledged kin to each other, as is so common in the South. Certainly, the Black Becnels weren't especially black, although none of those in my family could have passed for White.

Mildred Becnel came to nurse my sister, born in 1936. She stayed on to care for me, born three years later. Then she became our cook, and a marvelous cook she was. Over the years, after I left home, Mildred and I occasionally wrote to each other, so I know she was fairly literate, but she never cooked from recipes. Splendid Creole dishes— crawfish bisque, fricasseed chicken, stuffed crab, sweet and sour green beans, lemon icebox pie—all full of butter and salt, took form in her kitchen as if she were a sorceress. My parents' friends liked to dine at our house and not just for the company.

Mildred was my mother's age. Her sister Hilda, who came to work as a maid when I was about three, was a little older. She and Mildred were close and lived together when they weren't living with men. They were good-looking women, which I never noticed until I was grown. When my sister got married by chance Mildred wore the same dress to the wedding as my father's sister, and was by far the more striking. To my aunt's credit, she used to tell that story with great amusement.

When we had moved to a much larger house, Anna came to work as the laundress. She was the oldest of the Becnel siblings. I wasn't as close to her as I was to

Mildred and Hilda, partly because she had come after more of my life was focused outside the household, partly because she left much sooner, and partly because she worked in the basement, so I didn't see her during much of the day.

It was rare for a house in New Orleans to have a true basement—that is, one that was below ground level—because the city is below sea level and even the dead are buried in graves raised above ground. What were referred to as basements were the unfinished ground floors of houses called raised cottages, which had outside front steps leading up to a main entrance on the second floor. Because our basement was below ground, it was the most comfortable area of the house. It was cool in summer, in the days when air-conditioning was a novelty and even rooms with twelve-foot ceilings were warm, and it was cozy in winter because the oil-fired furnace was there.

Much later, Victorine, a fourth Becnel sister, for some years worked for my sister when Ann and her husband kept house in New Orleans for fifteen years before they moved to New York.

During the time I lived with my parents, the terms on which all our domestic help worked were economically exploitative. The hours were long, and the pay was low. They spent more time in our home than in their own. Things greatly improved after Title VII of the 1964 Civil Rights Act opened up a far wider range of employment opportunities for Black people. When Mildred and Hilda were in their sixties and seventies, their workdays were fewer each week and fairly short, and their real wages had improved. When first Hilda, then Mildred, turned eighty and retired, Mother settled a significant sum on each of them so they didn't have to live only on Social Security.

The happy Negro servant in the loving White family is a self-deluding myth. I nonetheless will affirm that the affection I had for Mildred and Hilda and theirs for me was genuine and lasted until their deaths. It helped that they knew of my views on, and involvement in, the Civil Rights Movement. But mostly it was because they had cared for me when I was a boy, and I made a point of keeping up the relationship all the years I no longer lived in New Orleans.

Two occasions from that long span of time come to mind. The first was when Hilda was over ninety and living in a nursing home. During one of the three visits I paid her there, I held her in my arms for thirty minutes while she cried. She was having a blue day. My last visit was more pleasant for me but not as tender.

To recount the other occasion will allow me to reach beyond the merely personal. There was one Becnel brother, Bud. As a young man, he had moved to Houston, where he held a low-paying but steady job at a country club until his retirement. Bud and his wife, Belgium, had two children, both of whom moved into the middle class, as did many of the next generation of Becnels. Robert became an attorney and Barbara Ann a nurse with the Veterans Administration.

Despite their children's success, when I moved to Houston in 1990, Bud and Belgium still were living in a run-down cottage just east of Houston's central business district. By 1999, Bud had died, and I had begun courting Deborah, my present wife. That May, Mildred let me know that she was coming to Houston to visit Belgium. Since Deborah was working for Shell Oil in one of the downtown office high-rises, I told Mildred I would bring Deborah to meet her so Mildred could decide whether she passed muster. She did.

It was Mildred's niece Rose who drove Mildred over from New Orleans. Rose's daughter was shortly to be married to a nephew of William Jefferson, the first Black to enter Congress from Louisiana since Reconstruction. He served nine terms beginning in 1991 then lost the House seat in the 2008 election after he had been indicted on sixteen felony counts related to corruption. His fall from grace is an all-too-common story in Louisiana politics. Jefferson's unique legacy is that he reinvested the phrase "cold cash" with its literal meaning when agents found $90,000 in the freezer of his Washington home. He served five years and some months in a federal penitentiary in Beaumont.

But at the time of Rose's visit, Jefferson was riding high, the most powerful figure in New Orleans politics. The family was excited about the engagement. Mom and Dad attended the wedding.

Beginning with my father's death in January 2001 at the age of ninety-six and ending with my mother's in June 2002 at age eighty-nine, all four of the people who had raised me passed away. After Dad, it was Hilda, then Mildred. I didn't need to seek closure with any of them as they neared death. I had spent decades of my adult life as friends with all four.

Still, several years later, an opportunity arose for me to effect what I considered a closing of the circle with Mildred and Hilda. Bud's son, Robert, had married a woman named

Nia, who taught in the School of Architecture at the University of Houston. Just before I moved to Houston, Nia had died of a blood disease. Because her scholarly work had focused on the preservation of the city's traditional Black neighborhoods, she was known and esteemed in the Black community. When the SHAPE Center, a major community organization in Houston's Third Ward, built its second facility, it was named after Nia Becnel.

In 2007, I was sentenced to fifty hours of community service stemming from a demonstration outside the Israeli Consulate. I arranged to do them at the SHAPE Center. On two occasions, I asked to mop the floors. The woman supervising me hesitated to agree. I was a sixty-eight-year-old retired college professor, and there were a number of much younger males doing community service there while I was. But I persisted, and she let me. I didn't explain to her that I wanted to mop the floors of a facility named after a member of the family that had mopped the floors of my home when I was a child. Even if I could have articulated my feelings, I'm certain they would have done me no credit in her estimation.

---

[1] Hodding III is the oldest son of Hodding II, former and long deceased publisher of the *Delta Democrat-Times* in Greenville, Mississippi. Before the Civil Rights Movement began, Hodding II took a relatively enlightened and very courageous stand on race relations. He was awarded a Pulitzer Prize in 1946 for his editorials. Ann Waldron's 1993 biography, *Hodding Carter: The Reconstruction of a Racist* (Algonquin Books), pays him the tribute that is his due. Philip, the second of three sons, entered Yale in 1957, the same year I did. We didn't know each other before then. Philip had grown up in Greenville, but he

had been born in New Orleans, and his mother, Betty Werlein Carter, was from a prominent family there. Which accounts for his being able to identify me as a New Orleanian when we spoke one evening outside the Yale Commons.

When Jimmy Carter became president, he appointed Hodding III Assistant Secretary of State for Public Affairs and State Department spokesman. The nation saw a lot of him during the Iran hostage crisis. Philip dropped out of Yale after one year, but he spent many of his subsequent years in the newspaper business in New Orleans, so we saw each other off and on. When I was the Democratic candidate for the Sixth Congressional District of Louisiana in 1984, he was kind enough to sink some money into that losing cause.

2  The founding father of the White Citizens' Council in Louisiana was State Senator William Rainach from Claiborne Parish in the north of the state, who led resistance to desegregation in the state legislature in the late 1950s. Earl Long, who served his third term as governor (non-consecutively, as then required) from 1956 to early 1960, would refer to Rainach as "Wee Willie, the apostle of hate." Like his deservedly more famous older brother, Huey, Earl did the best his times allowed to treat Black people fairly.

3  When a three-judge federal panel delivered its opinion in the case *of Sobol v. Perez* (1968), Judge Fred Ainsworth wrote, "The attitude in this parish toward realization by Negroes of their civil rights is well-known to this court. See *United States v. Plaquemines Parish School Board, supra*. District Attorney Leander Perez, Jr., stated publicly in 1965 that, if any known agitator were to appear in Plaquemines Parish, his mere presence would amount to a disturbance of the peace, since he was an outsider."

The full title of that case is *Richard B. SOBOL, Gary Duncan and Isaac Reynolds, Plaintiffs, v. Leander H. PEREZ, Sr.,*

*Leander H. Perez, Jr., District Attorney for the Twenty-Fifth Judicial District of Louisiana, and Eugene E. Leon, Judge of the Twenty-Fifth Judicial District of Louisiana, Defendants.* It stemmed from the legal defense of Gary Duncan, a Black resident of Plaquemines Parish, by a "known agitator" named Dick Sobol, who had come to Louisiana in fall 1966 under the auspices of the Lawyers Constitutional Defense Committee (LCDC). That case led to the landmark US Supreme Court decision in *Duncan v. Louisiana*, which established the right to trial by jury in all criminal cases when the sentence may include jail time. Leander had Dick arrested for practicing law without a license, even though he had been formally associated in Judge Leon's court with the New Orleans firm of Collins, Douglas, and Elie. For a history of those prosecutions and their outcomes, see the account by Vanderbilt law professor Nancy J. King, "The Story of *Duncan v. Louisiana*, 391 U.S. 145 (1968)," in *Criminal Procedure Stories*, edited by Carol Steiker (Eagan, MN: Foundation Press, 2006). In 2020, Little, Brown published *Deep Delta Justice*, Matthew Van Meter's book-length account of the *Duncan* case for the general reader.

Dick worked out of the ACLU office in New Orleans—LCDC was funded in large part by the national ACLU—but because he joined the law faculty at the University of Michigan in fall 1967, I only met him a few times. After he left Louisiana, Dick still continued to work on the cases that he had started there, including the extensive Title VII litigation against the giant paper company Crown Zellerbach at its plant in Bogalusa, Louisiana. Those several cases determined how the courts would implement the equal employment requirement of the 1964 Civil Rights Act, which was the great breakthrough for women as well racial and ethnic minorities. His Title VII work earned Dick an abiding place in US legal history.

# Chapter 2

# A Temple of the Holy Spirit

I spent 1965–1966, my first academic year at LSU, adjusting to my new situation. I was teaching too many courses, grading too many papers, trying to ready an article for publication, and waiting for a call I was certain would come.

It came that spring through William Armstrong Percy III. At that time, the History Department had its offices in the same building as the English Department. WAP, who was six years older than I, had joined that department a year before I arrived. He came from a distinguished literary family in Greenville, Mississippi, which included William Alexander Percy, poet and author of *Lanterns on the Levee*, and Walker Percy, who was raised by William Alexander after his own father committed suicide and whose great first novel, *The Moviegoer*, is set in New Orleans.[1]

Sometime in the spring, WAP stopped me in the hall to tell me that two leaders of the American Civil Liberties Union of Louisiana were coming up from New Orleans to get a chapter started in Baton Rouge. I had never heard of the ACLU, which wasn't as widely known then as it later became, but mainly because I was a political babe in the woods. When WAP, who was a member, briefly described the organization, I decided to attend the meeting.

I didn't know either Steve Rubin or Luis Zervigon, the two men who had come up. They were both about my age. Steve was teaching English at LSU-New Orleans. In 1964, he had led a wade-in to desegregate Pontchartrain Beach, a large amusement park and artificially created sand beach on the south shore of Lake Pontchartrain at the end of Elysian Fields Avenue. In keeping with the South's "separate but [un]equal" doctrine, for Blacks there was a far less developed amusement park called Lincoln Beach farther east along the lake shore. As a consequence of Steve's highly publicized activities, his car had been bombed. About a year after I met him, Steve moved back to New York. Luis was a New Orleans native, though, and he stayed.[2] We worked together frequently over the next few years.

Not many people attended the meeting that evening, but one was enough. I heard my call, and I answered it.

The meeting was held in the local office of the American Friends Service Committee. It was located in an old, poorly maintained one-story house on Government and Twelfth Street, appropriately close to what was then the borderline between a Black and a White neighborhood. The furnishings were shabby at best. But Marvin Resnikoff, rabbi at Liberal Synagogue, used to call it a Temple of the Holy Spirit.

The office was run by Wade Mackie, who worked for the American Friends Service Committee, the service arm of US Quakers. Along with the British Friends Service Council, the AFSC had been awarded the Nobel Peace

Prize in 1947. Wade had been posted to Louisiana in 1957, as the Civil Rights Movement was heating up. His specific assignment was to work for better job opportunities for Blacks but more generally to mobilize religious people to support love and justice with their deeds as well as their words. It was tough sledding. When he circulated among Baton Rouge clergy an "Affirmation of Basic Religious Principles," only two besides himself signed it. Marvin was one. The other was a Baptist minister named Irvin Cheney, whose congregation promptly dismissed him.

In 1961, the US attorney's office prosecuted Wendell Harris, then vice-chair of the State Sovereignty Commission, plus a second person, a private investigator, for illegally wiretapping Wade's office and home. Defending them in two trials that both ended in mistrials was Jack Rogers, who lived across the street from Wade's home. For a time, Rogers had a tap running from Wade's telephone box to his own garage, which was so obvious that Wade would laugh when he spoke of it.

As chief counsel of the Joint Louisiana Legislative Committee on Un-American Activities, Rogers hounded Wade diligently. Wade was called to be grilled by the committee, which, like J. Edgar Hoover and Leander Perez, was convinced that desegregation was a Communist plot. Nick Canaday told me that during the hearing, Wade was asked what Quakers had ever done for America. His laconic reply was, "Well, they founded Philadelphia."

That story was characteristic of Wade as well as his persecutors. He was a quiet man of rock-like integrity, never strident or bitter or resentful. People who knew him usually came to trust him, and bad as our performance on racial justice was, it would have been measurably worse without his twelve years of unswerving decency.

When Blacks and Whites met to break down barriers, chances were they met in the AFSC office. Chances were too that the police were outside writing down license plate numbers, a practice that I remember continued through 1968. But as then-East Baton Rouge Parish District Attorney Sergeant Pitcher pointed out when he was subpoenaed in connection with the federal wiretapping trials, it was against the law in Louisiana for members of the two races to meet together.

Wade helped me feel good about my work from its outset. That was important, because the dominant society could make those who challenged it from within feel bad about themselves. Good manners were a patina covering the ugly reality of Southern life, but most of us who grew up in that society had internalized them. It was one thing to openly oppose people like Jack Rogers. It was another to cause trouble for people like the university chancellor. They spoke in polite, reasonable, even friendly voices. If such people as these were in charge, could things really be bad enough to warrant disruptive behavior? They were.

My behavior was more disruptive than Wade's. He was at his best in gentle persuasion, not surprising for a Quaker. My family may have been genteel, but it was decidedly ungentle, and so whether by nurture or nature, I had what medieval Catholic theologians called an irascible soul—Thomas Aquinas associated it with daring and fear, hope and despair, and anger. I had lots of anger. The ACLU work allowed me to direct it to useful purposes. I was a scrapper and an increasingly skilled one. On the face of it, at least, I was a more effective change agent than Wade. I was not a better person.

The meeting I described earlier was the most important experience I had in Wade's office, but it wasn't the most memorable. That one occurred more than a year later on Halloween 1967.

What led to it was a recent decree by the Louisiana Legislature prohibiting the use of state money to bring Communist speakers to our public universities. Even at that late date, the suspicion, so widespread during the McCarthy era, that universities were a hotbed of Communism still lingered in Louisiana. The only conceivable ground for that suspicion was the Russian Studies program at LSU, a fledgling academic program that John Rarick, our US Representative at the time, publicly attacked and destroyed.[3]

A group of students who called themselves the Student Liberal Federation was determined to challenge the speaker ban. They were a bright and lively bunch and farther to the left than their organization's name implied. It took them two tries to break the ban. On the second, a man named Bubnov, who was the cultural attaché at the Soviet embassy in Washington, was allowed to speak. The poster they created for that event showed the red Soviet flag flying from the campus campanile. To my knowledge, there were no official repercussions, and like so much of the unconstitutional legislation the state's lawmakers passed in the sixties, the speaker ban died from disregard.

The students' first try had a different outcome. In October 1967, they invited Paul Boutelle, a Black taxi driver from Newark who was running for Vice President of the United States on the Socialist Workers Party ticket.

Boutelle was campaigning hard, touring the United States and appearing on national TV shows like William Buckley's and Dick Cavett's, in those days when the FCC's Fairness Doctrine gave voices beyond the mainstream a chance to be heard. He accepted the invitation to come to Baton Rouge.

At first, Chancellor Cecil "Pete" Taylor ruled that Boutelle couldn't speak on campus. Under pressure, at the last minute, he came up with the foolish proposal that Boutelle could speak if he shared the platform with a man who ran the local John Birch Society book store. Boutelle, who by then had arrived in town, declined, saying he had received an invitation to speak in another venue. It turned out that Wade had offered to let him use the AFSC office.

These events were attracting significant news coverage. So the night of the talk, which was Halloween, about three hundred people showed up. Wade's office was packed, and people stood outside listening through open windows. Boutelle began by excoriating the United States for the war in Vietnam. This was a guaranteed crowd-pleaser. The morality and wisdom of the war were still hotly contested subjects in Baton Rouge and far beyond, but the people in attendance that night, mostly students under the cloud of the draft, had made up their minds.

Boutelle's rhetoric was more radical than I had ever heard. I remember his holding up a small flag and calling it the American rag. He made me nervous, but he also thrilled me. The terrible destruction our nation had unleashed on the Vietnamese people was unconscionable, and it seemed right to be unsparing in our criticism.

Having spent about fifteen minutes on the issues, including racism, Boutelle turned to Marxist analysis. He was intelligent and articulate but pedagogical, and the audience's attention quickly lapsed. Some forty-five minutes later, he suggested that we take a short break. The attendance thinned dramatically.

That was fortunate. Just after Boutelle resumed his presentation, a lit fuse came through a window. I threw myself on the floor behind an old couch and waited for the explosion. None came. When I looked up, Boutelle hadn't moved. After we had recollected ourselves, he resumed his talk. I don't know whether he was courageous or foolhardy, but in fact, there was nothing he could have done to save himself had it been a bomb rather than a malicious prank.

The old house was torn down sometime after I left Baton Rouge in 1987; I don't know when. I do know more precisely the fate of the man whose spirit led Marvin to call it a temple. In 1969, Wade and his wife Selma left Baton Rouge and moved into a Quaker retirement community in North Carolina. He died in 1971.

This recollection is my third opportunity to keep Wade's memory alive in Baton Rouge.

The first occurred in 1980, when I was writing a weekly column in the Baton Rouge Sunday Advocate at the invitation of Douglas Manship Sr., the publisher. In my third column, I celebrated the courageous work of Wade and Marvin, who had also died by then, and Father Elmer Powell, a Black Catholic priest who had been Bishop Robert Tracy's point person on race relations and the de-segregation of diocesan institutions. Apparently, there was some reluctance to publish the column; the managing editor asked me to make some changes, but I refused, and it ran.

The second was when I successfully proposed to the board of the Center for Disarmament Education, later renamed Bienville House Center for Peace and Justice, that we institute an award in Wade's name. A brief tribute to Wade and a list of the annual recipients can be found on the Bienville House website.

The Center was founded on my initiative in 1978 after I became alarmed over Jimmy Carter's failure to reverse the nuclear arms race. I guided it to stability in its early years, and it has endured.

My change of focus from civil liberties to disarmament and peace work had a salutary effect on my personal growth. One shouldn't work for the ACLU if one isn't comfortable with, even disposed to, conflict, usually win-lose conflicts, but I often would have been more effective had I possessed the skills of peaceful communication I learned much later. Nonetheless, anger is a spur to justice, and the world would probably be a finer place if there were a larger collective capacity for righteous anger.

Still, I needed to realize that, at a deep level, I was angry all the time and that my anger had nothing to do with the world and everything to do with my personal life starting when I was a boy. Peacemaking requires that we sort out and resolve those internal conflicts that prevent us from modeling the attitude and behaviors that we are urging the world to adopt on a larger scale.

My internal journey from violence to wholeness has been long and isn't yet complete. On that journey, my memory of Wade's witness has been a resource. I don't think it too great a stretch to claim that he set up office within me.

---

[1] But WAP was ill at ease in a Southern university. Somewhere along the line he, like me, had had a change of mind about the culture in which he was raised. And he was gay, a fact he understandably tried to hide. An embarrassing episode forced him to leave LSU soon after the event I'm recounting. He finally felt secure enough to come out of the closet when he gained tenure at UMass-Boston in 1975. By that time—indeed earlier—it would have been safe for him to come out at LSU as well. Students for Gay Awareness had formed and been officially recognized as a campus organization. I was proud to be its first faculty advisor.

[2] I soon learned that Luis was married to Mary Keller, the older sister of a classmate of mine at Isidore Newman School and daughter of Rosa Freeman Keller. The Freemans were a wealthy family—they owned the Coca Cola bottling franchise—and wielded influence in the city. Working within the civic structure, Rosa had done important work to advance race relations, and her daughters were sympathetic to racial justice.

[3] Rarick had been a district judge in West Feliciana Parish just upriver from Baton Rouge before he won the Sixth Congressional District seat in 1966, narrowly defeating longtime moderate Democrat Jimmy Morrison in the Democratic primary by playing the race card. He had also been a member of the White Citizens' Council. In Congress, Rarick quickly became notorious. Even by Republican standards of the time, to say nothing of his own party's, he was beyond the pale. He lost the seat in 1975, and while he tried to stay alive politically—among other efforts, in 1980 he ran for president as the nominee of the American Independent Party, founded by George Wallace when

Wallace ran for president in 1968—he was finished. Rarick spent his remaining years (d. 2009) practicing law back home in St. Francisville. After my oldest son, Jesse, moved to West Feliciana in the 1990s, he joined a long-running social poker game that included Rarick. When "the judge," as he was habitually called, would make racist comments, Jesse said that the other players would just tell him to cool it. Jesse grew rather fond of the aging and increasingly feckless man and rendered him some service after Rarick's wife predeceased him. I'm glad he did. Kindness is rarely misplaced.

# CHAPTER 3

# "Confused Alarums of Struggle"

It was a year after I founded the ACLU chapter in Baton Rouge in fall 1966 that we made our first big splash. Construction of the new East Baton Rouge Parish prison, out by the airport, had been completed, but prisoners hadn't yet been transferred to it. A colleague in the Philosophy Department told me that a man he knew had been the subcontractor for some of the internal wiring and that he had been directed to install bugs in the two lawyer-client consultation rooms. He asked if I wanted the plans.

He needn't have asked.

When I got the rolled-up bundle, it made me nervous. I was young (28) and young at the work, so I couldn't make a realistic assessment of the risk. I stored the plans in a locker at the downtown bus station.

Then I had the good sense to seek advice from Sam D'Amico, a respected criminal defense attorney in town. "Mr. Sam" lived down the street from our home on Glenmore Avenue. He and I met in his living room. When I told him what I knew, he simply picked up the telephone and called the sheriff, Bryan Clemmons, who by Louisiana law was in charge of the parish penal facilities. Clemmons denied the accusation and invited D'Amico and me to come out to the prison the next day and inspect the facility.

After teaching my morning classes, I retrieved the plans and drove out to the prison. Clemmons and D'Amico were there, and so were the media. TV crews followed us down the hall with their cameras on big dollies. My stomach was churning.

We entered one of the rooms. It was small with a metal table and two facing metal chairs bolted to the floor. Clemmons rather smugly asked me to point out the bugs, suggesting that I look under the table. I pointed to the acoustic panels in the dropped ceiling and asked that some of them be removed. A reporter from Channel 9, the CBS affiliate, stood on the table and pushed aside a panel. There were wires dangling from a box in the true ceiling. When I asked where they led, Clemmons admitted it was to a deputy station at the front of the prison.

I felt more relief than triumph. When I returned to campus, the story had already been on TV. Then the afternoon newspaper came out. The story began on the front page under the headline, "Rothschild Finds No Bugs in the Jail." But the story made it abundantly clear that the headline was correct only in the narrowest sense that the listening devices had either not yet been installed or had been removed before I arrived. Accompanying the runover on page 3 was a photograph of the Channel 9 reporter standing on the table with the wires dangling down.[1]

Later, the wires themselves were pulled out.

\*\*\*\*\*

Not long thereafter, I found myself sitting in one of those rooms across the steel table from a middle-aged Black man. Why his jailors allowed me to visit him I don't know; I wasn't an attorney and they could have denied me access.

A letter from the prison to the ACLU chapter's post office box had brought me to the meeting. The letter was signed with the man's name, but I quickly realized that another inmate must have written it. The man seemed barely articulate verbally, and the letter had laid out clearly enough the relevant facts of his situation.

They had upset me.

He had been arrested and charged with a crime fourteen years before, but he hadn't been prosecuted. Instead, he had been sent to the forensic unit at East Louisiana State Hospital in Jackson, a town in the adjacent parish of East Feliciana.

People tend to believe that forensic units in state hospitals are for people who escape conviction by successfully pleading innocent by reason of insanity. Not so the one at East. It was very hard to make an insanity plea in Louisiana. The forensic unit at East was largely a holding pen for pretrial detainees.

The only proper legal basis for sending someone to a mental institution before trial is because that person is too mentally disturbed to understand the charges or assist counsel in his/her defense. But we hadn't yet established that standard in Louisiana. In practice, a district attorney could transfer anyone whom he claimed, without a judicial showing, was mentally disturbed.[2]

That was a convenient way to keep people locked up without a trial. I subsequently communicated with a person who had been held in East for seventeen years and, later, another who had been held twenty-one years. Still later, I read in the paper of the release of someone after fifty years. How they didn't go stark raving mad under such circumstances still amazes me.[3]

As we were talking, the man expressed mild annoyance at my several requests to repeat what he was saying. I felt badly about that. But under any circumstances, it wouldn't have been easy for a White city boy like me to understand a Black man raised in rural Mississippi. And his ability to communicate must have deteriorated during his twelve years at East and then two more in parish prison after his return.

Which was an *autre chose encore*, as my mother would say. How could he have just sat in prison for two years when in all probability the state couldn't make a case against him after all those years, if it ever could have? There was, I soon discovered, an answer to that question. The attorney the court had appointed to represent him on his return from East had done nothing whatsoever in all that time.

The parish had no public defender office then. Representation of indigent defendants was assigned on a rotating basis among Baton Rouge lawyers. This man's case had been assigned to Bill Norfolk, who worked for the largest firm in the city, Taylor, Porter, Fuller, and Phillips.

In the short time I had been running the ACLU chapter, I had seen a good bit of injustice, but I wasn't prepared for what I had just heard in the prison. Things like that didn't happen to people like me, who had grown up and gone through school among mostly wealthy people. We had too much money, too much social position, too many connections, to just disappear as this man had done. I was shocked, and I was angry. And the immediate focus of my anger was Bill Norfolk, whose name I was to learn within a couple of days.

I called him. Apparently, he had gotten word that the ACLU had become interested because he told me he had filed papers for the man's release. "That's good," I said, "but why didn't you do that two years ago?"

"I don't have to answer to you," he said angrily.

"Maybe you do," I said, and we hung up.

I sent a letter to the Louisiana Bar Association on ACLU chapter stationery, laid out the facts as I knew them, and asked them to disbar Norfolk. I had no expectation that the folks there would even look into the case, but they did. After a length of time I no longer remember, I received a letter saying that while *I* might have handled the case differently, Norfolk's conduct was within reasonable standards of client representation.

Not long after, I was having coffee at the LSU Faculty Club with George Pugh and Mike Klein, two members of the law school faculty. Mike was about my age, George considerably older. When I spoke of the letter I had received from the bar, George said he thought the ruling was a correct one. Mike asked him, "What do you think *would* be grounds for disbarment?"

"Stealing a client's money," George answered.

"He stole two years of that man's life," I said.

That same year East Baton Rouge Parish established a public defender office. I was told that the impetus came from the city's large law firms. But it pleases me to believe that the impetus came from a poor Black man from Mississippi...and me.

*****

That experience convinced me that the consequences of action in the public arena are unpredictable and, to a large extent, unknowable. I came to believe that if my motive was decent and the goal worthwhile, more good than harm would ensue despite the limits of my knowledge and abilities. That article of faith was more fundamental to my life than those in the Nicene Creed, which at that time I was reciting each Sunday.

From time to time, some of the unforeseen consequences of my work did manifest themselves—usually to my satisfaction, occasionally to my chagrin. Three occasions besides the one I just recounted now come to mind: desegregating the Baton Rouge YWCA, reforming the Louisiana Legislature, and throwing mentally ill persons onto the streets. The stories of the first two follow in this chapter. I'll tell the third story in Chapter 7.

*****

In 1966, the local YMCA and YWCA were still segregated by race. It hadn't occurred to me to look into that situation until a former student contacted me in early 1967 to say that she had brought some school children to the YMCA to swim and the Black children hadn't been allowed in. I visited the director at the facility. We talked by the pool. He said, in what seemed to me a pained tone, that it would simply be impossible for him to support desegregation of his facility. I knew what he meant—those White families splashing around in front of us would rather have no pool at all than share it with "coloreds." The city had already closed some of its pools rather than maintain them as integrated facilities.[4]

My recourse was to contact the national office of the Y. I sent off a letter calling attention to the local situation and urging intervention. Not long thereafter, I received a reply, not from the national YMCA but from the national YWCA. The letter stated an intention to act.

I can only guess what had happened. In those days before the Internet, we relied on telephone books to get addresses. The LSU library kept directories for large cities in the United States, and doubtless I used one of them— probably the Washington, DC directory, which is where the YWCA, but not the YMCA, was headquartered. I had been careless.

The Baton Rouge YWCA was founded in 1943 to serve White women and girls. Local Black women formed the Maggie Nance Ringgold Unit of the YWCA eleven years later. In 1965, the national YWCA convention mandated that all YWCAs in the country be racially integrated. Of course, in the South that wasn't going to happen voluntarily. At the time of my misdirected letter, the Baton Rouge YWCA maintained two separate and very unequal facilities.

Action by the national office put an end to that—in a manner of speaking only. The White Christian women of the local Y came together at a meeting at which the Black members were not allowed to vote, and they withdrew from the national. They adopted the name YWCO (O for Organization as distinguished from A for Association) and kept the nicer facility.

A few White members didn't go along. They remained members of an integrated but now predominantly Black YWCA, which was chartered as *the* local YWCA by the national organization that same year. I wish I could preserve all the names of the Whites who refused to secede. I only remember one of them because she was a friend. Honoring her must serve to honor them all.

Her name was Doucette Pascal. That's the name by which I got to know her because I met her many years after she had married Robert Pascal, a professor at the LSU Law School. But she delighted in remembering me as Sonny Rothschild in short pants when she was Doucette Cherbonnet and teaching science at Isidore Newman School in New Orleans. My sister, three years older than I, had been her student. Doucette married Bob and moved to Baton Rouge shortly before I would have entered her class.

Both Doucette and Bob befriended my wife and me. I appreciated them. They were highly intelligent, interesting and kind, and both were committed to racial justice. They were Roman Catholics, and they believed that their faith required it of them. Doucette was a strong voice calling on a foot-dragging Bishop Robert Tracy to integrate diocesan schools and churches.

According to the current website of the Baton Rouge YWCA, the YWCO eventually disbanded. The few remains of that disgraceful institution are old copies of *C'est si bon*, the cookbook it published as a fundraiser in 1969.

*****

I'm not sure how the Louisiana Legislature conducts itself now, but when I was a volunteer lobbyist for the state ACLU, it was anything but a professional body. One of its practices that bothered good government activists was allowing lobbyists on the floor while official business, including voting, was being conducted. Ending that practice had been a long-standing goal of the Public Affairs Research Council of Louisiana (PAR). I hadn't given the matter much thought and doubt that I would have cared much if I had. So neither PAR nor I could have predicted that I would put the winning card in its hand.

What I cared very much about, going into the 1970 session, were two bills for which we had found sponsors. Both would amend the Louisiana Code of Criminal Procedure. One would make it mandatory, not discretionary, for a criminal court judge to give credit for time served before sentencing a convicted defendant. The other would require speedy appearance before a judge following arrest.

Dale E. Bennett, a professor at the LSU Law School, was the person most responsible for the iteration of the code adopted in 1966. Bennett was highly admired for his contributions to criminal law in the state. When he retired in 1975, the fall issue of the LSU Law Review was dedicated to him, and in the dedication, then-dean Paul M. Hebert called him "Mr. Criminal Law of Louisiana." I'm not in a position to gainsay such a tribute. I only read those portions of the code that applied to the situations I investigated. They were unconducive to justice.

That the code didn't mandate credit for time served before sentencing was patently unjust. I suspected that the district attorneys had pressured Bennett into a shoddy compromise because making credit discretionary fed into another injustice that served their purpose well—namely, to use it as leverage to compel guilty pleas. If a person is sitting in jail day after day awaiting a day in court, the offer of credit for time served can be tempting.

Just how long might a person wait between arrest and first court appearance? The code didn't answer that question; it prescribed no limit. How long wasn't a matter of law, I discovered, but of practice.

Not only was the code silent on this matter, but it was also defective. In it, the first appearance was the arraignment, which is the occasion when defendants enter their pleas to the charges. But by 1966, thanks to the landmark US Supreme Court decision in *Gideon v. Wainwright* three years earlier, all defendants in felony prosecutions were entitled to legal defense and a court-appointed attorney if they couldn't afford to hire their own. This meant that in such cases, a plea couldn't be entered without the assistance of counsel. So poor defendants' first appearance no longer was an arraignment but the occasion when the judge would ask if they needed court-appointed counsel. If they did, the real arraignment was set for a still later date.

The federal code by that time had what was called "appearance before a magistrate," a procedure preceding arraignment. It struck me as a model worth adopting.

Along with assuring that poor defendants get legal advice prior to entering their pleas, their first court appearance is also a time when a judge can set a bail appropriate to their cases. At time of arrest, in Louisiana bail was automatically set by a fixed schedule related to the severity of the charges, and for even minor crimes, the amounts were often beyond the means of poor defendants. But the legitimate purpose of bail is to assure the defendants' appearance at their court dates after release, and the seriousness of their alleged offenses is but one consideration. More important are their life circumstances. Persons with deep roots in the community are not much of a flight risk despite the seriousness of the charges, especially if they are poor. So the sooner defendants can come before a magistrate to make known the particulars of their situations, the more likely they are to get their bonds lowered to levels they or their families can make and thus resume their lives pending the outcome of their cases. The federal code went far to facilitate this outcome. The Louisiana code in effect assured that large numbers of poor defendants spent considerable time in jail no matter the eventual outcomes of their cases.[5]

Again, how long would a person in Louisiana have to wait before first appearance after arrest? The appeals for help I was getting in the "jail mail" had led me to ask that question. Sometime in 1968, I set out to answer it.

The first answer I got was about East Baton Rouge Parish. There, a person could wait as many as six to eight weeks. I subsequently learned that in other parishes it was as long as six months. The longest delays were in sparsely populated rural parishes that shared a lone judge with neighboring parishes.[6]

Pressured by us, in 1969 Sargent Pitcher, the district attorney for East Baton Rouge Parish, set a week as the maximum time a person would be held before court appearance. But I also wanted to get a standard set for the entire state. So I got the state ACLU board to support filing a bill that would require speedy appearance after arrest—we started with a four-day maximum, failing which the person must be released. As the bill made its way through the process, it got amended to set a seven-day maximum—not good, but a major improvement over existing practices.

At that time, the legislature conducted its general sessions in the even numbered years, with shorter and exclusively fiscal sessions in the odd years. And the general sessions are short—sixty meeting days within an eighty-five-day period. Several thousand bills are filed, and getting any one of them all the way through the process before term expires is difficult unless it has powerful backers.

By the last day of the 1970 session, mandatory credit for time served had made it through. To my delight, both chambers also had passed our speedy appearance bill in its amended form, even though the district attorneys association, which wields enormous clout, didn't like it. Unfortunately, the Senate version differed from the House version, so it had to go back to the lower chamber. The differences weren't substantive, so if the bill got to a vote, it would surely pass. On that "if" hung my hopes.

As that last day wore on, I left the capitol. Two other ACLU volunteers stayed until the midnight adjournment, and one of them filled me in on the outcome the following day. Time had run out on us; the bill died for lack of final approval.

Though that was the sad gist of his report, it wasn't the whole of it. A representative from New Orleans, Sal Anselmo, had taken a liking to Linda Watkins, our other volunteer on the scene. Sal was a smart and dedicated legislator, unlike many of his colleagues. So as many of them called it quits, the attrition beginning at suppertime, Sal stayed on and attended to business. He kept Linda by his desk. As bills came up for disposition, he told Linda to help him get to the desks of absent colleagues and press their voting buttons as he directed. Presumably, they had authorized him to cast their votes, but I have no way of knowing that. This activity lasted until the session ended.

When I wrote the wrap-up story on the legislative session for the state ACLU newsletter, I included that account simply because I thought it entertaining. I'm not sure I would have shared it had I thought that anyone but ACLU members read the newsletter. Not long afterward, I discovered my error. The PAR newsletter ran a front-page article renewing its call for banning anyone but legislators from the floor when official business was being conducted. As evidence for the need, it quoted what I had written about Anselmo and Watkins.

That proved determinative. There's no way of knowing whether legislators were more upset that voting buttons were pushed when members weren't present or that they were pushed by someone from the ACLU. Whichever or both, it was beyond the pale. By 1972, all but legislators had to leave the floor when official business began.

And in the session that year, enough legislators pushed their own voting buttons in favor of our speedy appearance bill that it at last became law.

---

[1] Largely because the size and length of headlines are determined by page layout, over which reporters have no say, they don't write the headlines for their stories. Others write them for their stories as well as for wire service feeds. This arrangement affords an opportunity for editorializing in the news section, which by journalistic canon is supposedly forbidden. At the time of this incident, the *State-Times* was more conservative—meaning, among other things, more racist—than the *Morning Advocate*, even though they both were published by the Manship family's Capital City Press. The editor of the *State-Times* was C. C. Brown, an unreconstructed Southerner. When circumstances threw us together in 1984, years after he had retired, he told me ruefully, "I don't recognize my own paper anymore." The Manships stopped publishing the *State-Times* in 1991.

[2] Nonetheless, in 1970, Joe W. Sanders, then a Louisiana Supreme Court justice and chairman of the Louisiana Commission on Law Enforcement and the Administration of Criminal Justice, told the Louisiana Association for Mental Health, "At this time, I have no changes in the law to recommend" (summer 1970 issue of *Target*, the LAMH newsletter). Three years later, Sanders would become Chief Justice.

[3] In Chapter 7 ("Commitments"), I tell the story of our protracted work to bring due process to the civil commitment of the mentally ill in Louisiana. Criminal commitment is an entirely different process with entirely different legal and practical motives. It also affected far fewer people but constituted a grave injustice. I persuaded the ACLU of Louisiana, of which I was president (1970–1972), and the

Louisiana Association for Mental Health, on whose Public Affairs Committee I served (1969–1972), to address the injustice. On June 18, 1971, Luke Fontana filed suit for the state ACLU to close the forensic unit at East Louisiana State Hospital, the only such unit in the state. The suit ultimately failed, but it created pressure for change.

Broad relief finally came in the 1975 legislative session. It mandated that

- the process be placed under court supervision from the start;
- appointment of counsel for defendants if they had none before the process could go forward;
- appointment of a sanity commission within seven days of the motion to declare incompetence to stand trial, but that didn't deprive defendants of the right to an independent mental examination by a physician or mental health expert of their choice;
- the sanity commission to report its findings to the court within thirty days; and
- an evidence-based court hearing on competence, with both the prosecution and defense authorized to call and to cross-examine witnesses.

The new statute specified what would happen if the court ruled that a defendant was incompetent. Those articles of the code are complex, varying with prognosis of success of treatment and also the severity of the charge. Suffice it to say here that defendants can never be hospitalized for longer than the sentences they would have received if convicted, and it is unlikely that they can ever be lost from court supervision. See Articles 641-649.1 Louisiana Code of Criminal Procedure.

[4] Before passage of the 1964 Civil Rights Act, which mandated integration of public facilities, there was one pool used

exclusively by Blacks, which had been built and maintained by a Black non-profit association. The public pools had all been reserved for Whites. The city then closed its pools located in areas of the city that were likely to be used by both races. In spring, 1966 two of those pools—one in Howell Park and the other in Webb Park—which had reopened as integrated facilities, were bombed. The pumping and filtration systems were badly damaged, and by 1970, they still hadn't been reopened.

5  In this context, it is worth noting that at least 40 percent of persons arrested and charged with serious felonies have their cases dismissed either at pretrial screening or by the court (see, for example, Boland, Logan, Sones, and Martin, "The Prosecution of Felony Arrests, 1982," US Department of Justice, Bureau of Justice Statistics, May 1988, NJC-I06990). The percentage of dismissals in misdemeanor cases is probably much higher and the likelihood of jail sentences if convicted much lower. Thus, many people were serving significant jail time who could not or would not have been sentenced to it.

6  In 1968, to get the data for East Baton Rouge Parish, I sought the help of Mike Klein at the law school. He recruited a few students to go to the jail and examine the book at the admitting desk. The jail book by law must contain information about when a person is jailed, on what charge, when he appears in court, when he is freed or transferred, and, in the latter case, where to. Also by law, anyone can examine the book. These requirements are safeguards against secret detention. But the students were denied access. Mike had to send two letters to Sheriff Clemmons to get his cooperation. The statewide study was done by others at the law school. Sheriffs in other parishes must have supplied the data themselves.

# CHAPTER 4

## Struggles in My Workplace

When I retired from LSU after the 1987 summer term, it was a much finer academic institution than when I arrived for fall term 1965. I attribute the improvement to three principal causes.

Perhaps most important was that the sellers' market for new PhDs turned into a buyers' market at the end of the 1960s. Across the country enrollment growth was slowing dramatically because the demographic bulge we learned to call the Baby Boomers was already in or beyond college. But universities were still producing new PhDs in accelerating numbers. Reduction of graduate program enrollments lagged well behind reduced undergraduate enrollments.[1] So new PhDs from the best graduate schools were applying for tenure-track positions at LSU and in many cases felt fortunate if they were hired.

Second was a radical change in the aspirations of our female students. Title VII of the 1964 Civil Rights Act, which forbade discrimination in employment based on gender as well as race, religion, and national origin, took only a few years to open a wide new range of workplace opportunities for college-educated women. Before, only nursing and elementary and high school teaching employed large numbers, and pay was low in those years before teachers, and later, nurses acquired power by unionizing.

The undergraduate student body at LSU was largely middle class. To risk a generalization that I think contains much truth, families that didn't want their daughters to enter the workforce after high school as retail clerks and secretaries sent them to LSU, where their expectation was to meet an eligible mate prior to graduation. Given that motive for college-going, our female students contributed as much to campus social life as to academic life. A perennially successful football team and a well-developed fraternity and sorority system helped LSU maintain its reputation as a party school.

It was our female students who changed the tenor of undergraduate life. Once they saw the possibility of taking economic control of their futures, academic success gained an urgency it had previously lacked. Not many years into my career at LSU, I perceived that in the aggregate, women were more serious and dedicated students than their male counterparts. That trend nationally has never been reversed. Females are enjoying significantly more academic success than males.

The third reason that LSU improved so much during my twenty-two years there was political. The quality of a public university cannot exceed by much the quality of the polity to which it is accountable. As long as Louisiana was a closed society, open-ended inquiry, vigorous discussion, and cultivation of critical intelligence were muted in its institutions of higher learning. Some of them—including the historically Black schools—were explicitly repressive. That wasn't true of LSU, although certain campus regulations of First Amendment exercise had to be challenged. But almost all the students and many of the faculty and administrators had been formed by the prevailing culture, and they set the tone simply by being who they were. The most unreconstructed faculty were in departments closely linked to state government—the colleges of Agriculture and Education.

As the Civil Rights Movement, the turmoil over the Vietnam War, and the new youth culture impacted society in general, so too the tenor of life at LSU changed. Students chafed under the personal restrictions that marked the *in loco parentis* paradigm for the school-student relationship. Their rebellion also focused on the two years of compulsory ROTC for all entering male students. Faculty who grew up or had studied outside the South became more vocal, and our numbers increased as faculty hiring became a buyers' market. Ten years after my arrival, the civil liberties issues and the blatant racial problems on campus had largely been resolved.

*****

The first case that came to me after I formed the Baton Rouge Chapter of the ACLU of Louisiana concerned a deaf man who was teaching at the Louisiana School for the Deaf, then located in downtown Baton Rouge. He was a recent graduate of Gallaudet University, the federally chartered private university for the hearing impaired located in Washington, DC. As such, he hadn't taken all the courses required for teacher certification in Louisiana. That situation wasn't unusual. The way the state handled it was to grant a temporary (T) certificate, which could be maintained as long as its holder took six hours of coursework at an accredited Louisiana university toward completion of certification requirements. There were two universities in Baton Rouge, LSU and Southern, but LSU was an easy bus ride from the School for the Deaf, whereas Southern was quite distant and not easily accessed by public transportation. So the young man applied to our College of Education. He was refused admission on the ground that he was deaf. Most people would have regarded deafness as a strong qualification for teaching the hearing impaired, but it violated the admissions standards of the college.

Actually, the College of Education ran the only undergraduate program at LSU that had admissions standards beyond what the university had. It would allow any student to take a few introductory courses but not enough courses to qualify for state certification. For that, a student had to be vetted. This unique power should not have been tolerated by the rest of the university, but until 1971 it was.[2]

So what were its admissions standards? I learned the answer when I spoke with Nick Canaday, my English Department colleague, about the case. He pulled out a copy of the printed version of a 1961 talk that Lemos Fulmer, the dean, had given to a group of townspeople. The focus of his talk was how his college made sure that only presentable people got into Louisiana schoolrooms. As an example, Fulmer cited the college's rejection of a student with a red beard. "I do not feel that, in most instances, we would find a person of that type to possess the emotional stability which we desire in our teachers." In the same speech, Fulmer explained, "If a faculty member [from anywhere in the university] discovers something about a student that would be detrimental to the profession, it can be reported to the Retention Committee." What was especially egregious about this arbitrary and capricious screening of those fit to teach was that the upper administration tolerated it, like Catholic bishops tolerating pederasty in their dioceses. I welcomed the opportunity to expose it to judicial scrutiny and public condemnation. Unfortunately, our plaintiff chose to leave Louisiana for a job elsewhere. The College of Education's separate admissions requirement was dropped after John L. Garrett became dean, but neither the culture nor the academic quality of the college started changing significantly until Peter Soderbergh was brought in as dean from the University of Virginia.[3]

LSU had a K-12 school, the University Laboratory School, nominally as part of the College of Education. The faculty were also LSU faculty appointments. To my knowledge, no research based on work at the "Lab School" was ever published (for that matter, under Fulmer's leadership, the entire college faculty published very little). So the school's name was a cover for its real purpose, which was to provide a private school experience at public expense to the children of well-placed families, both at LSU and in the larger community. It was common for elected officials who wished to claim that they sent their kids to public school to enroll them in the Lab School.

In the late 1960s, anticipating that the school's admissions policy would be challenged on the ground of racial discrimination, the school admitted a handful of Black students from professional families. That, however, was not why we in the ACLU chapter were moved in 1971 to challenge the school's restrictive admissions policy. Rather, the policy wasn't serving any legitimate academic mission. Quite the opposite. Even if research and teacher training were being done to further the quality of high school teaching, the Lab School wasn't assembling a student body representative of students in the public school district, much less selecting for students who present the largest challenges to successful teaching. Thus, in our view, its restrictive admissions violated equal protection of the law.

We didn't think we could mount a court challenge because of the difficulty of finding a plaintiff. Instead, we decided to mobilize pressure for change by exposing the problem publicly. Michael Dollinger, an assistant professor in the Mathematics Department, volunteered to document the discrimination. Using the Lab School's yearbooks to identify the livelihoods of the parents of the students, then using an academically-established scale to display the socioeconomic status of those livelihoods, Dollinger documented our claim in persuasive detail. We released the report to the news media, and the *Baton Rouge Morning Advocate*, the leading daily, ran the story on the front page of its next Sunday edition. That sent shockwaves through the LSU administration, but no major changes in admissions took place until Soderberg became dean.[4]

\*\*\*\*\*

Race and, to a lesser extent, gender were the primary bases of illegitimate discrimination by the university. This was less true of the student body than it was of the faculty and staff because one of Huey P. Long's populist legacies was permission for anyone who graduated from an accredited Louisiana high school to attend any state institution of higher education. LSU had long been coed, and there were no institutional barriers to the admission of Blacks once legally mandated segregation ended in 1964. That year, six Black undergraduates matriculated without the turmoil that had accompanied the integration of the University of Mississippi (1962) and the University of Alabama (1963).[5] How much those pioneering Black students had to endure I don't know; no harassment or discrimination came to my attention. In spring, 1972, Kerry Pourciau, an African American student, was elected president of the Student Government Association.[6]

Black student enrollment increased slowly, and the percentage of Blacks at LSU has never approximated their percentage of the state's population. In the fall of 2018, they constituted only 12 percent of the 31,000 students. I don't believe this underrepresentation is a function of a hostile environment. Ever since the university's football and basketball teams finally integrated, Black students' acceptance on campus has been secure.[7] One explanation for the underrepresentation is that Southern University is a more attractive choice, especially for academically underprepared students, which unfortunately remains the case of graduates from the *de facto* segregated school systems of New Orleans and Baton Rouge, which are the primary geographic feeder areas of LSU undergraduates. And a predominantly Black environment may simply be more congenial.

In 1965, the faculty was unintegrated racially. Its first Black faculty member was Julian T. White, hired as a professor of architecture in 1971. At that time, the US Department of Labor and the Department of Health, Education, and Welfare had begun pressuring universities to diversify their faculties by race and by gender. One of their more effective tactics was to require submission of a report whenever a tenure-track position was filled. The report asked about Blacks and women in the applicant pool, and if there had been any and a White male nevertheless had been hired, it required a demonstration of his decisively better qualifications. As institutions responded to such pressure, it became very difficult to hire African Americans, because the pool of Black PhDs was small and universities in the South were hardly their most attractive opportunities. To their credit, the feds understood that reality and mainly pressured us to hire women.

I was on sabbatical during the 1972–1973 academic year. Upon my return, the chair of the English Department asked me to be affirmative action officer, an unofficial position unique to our department within the university. It carried no released time from teaching, so along with my extracurricular ACLU work, it left almost no time for research and publication. I served in that capacity for two years, during which I had to sit on every search committee and read every applicant's packet. But the results were rewarding. Before, we had only one woman in the professoriate. We added three more, who all had strong careers subsequently. And the trend toward diversification continued. Before I left LSU in 1987, we had many women in tenured or tenure-track positions and had even managed to hire three Blacks at that level.

Actually, there had been no shortage of women on the faculty before federal pressure for gender diversity began, but they were clustered at the rank of instructor. At one time, all beginning faculty in US universities started as instructors, but by the mid-sixties, the beginning rank for holders of the PhD was assistant professor. Instructors were almost always without doctorates.[8] At LSU, the large service departments, mainly English, Mathematics, and Foreign Languages, employed the most instructors because they didn't have enough graduate teaching assistants to staff the lower-level courses that were prerequisites of all or many majors.

The conditions of employment and continued employment for instructors were unregularized when I arrived. Many were given a full teaching load (twelve hours) and, with it, benefits. Others, sometimes by choice, sometimes not, only taught part-time and received no benefits. The only job security was LSU's willingness to honor the rule of the American Association of University Professors (AAUP) that any contract for a seventh year of continuous employment that didn't include notice of termination after the completion of that year meant de facto tenure. A sizable number of female instructors in my department had achieved de facto tenure, and a very small number of those had been promoted to assistant professor, the highest rank they could achieve. But none of them participated in faculty meetings.

Besides their legally shaky and marginalized standing, the fate of instructors was largely in the hands of the departmental administrator responsible for staffing the service courses. In my department that was the Chair of Freshman English. There was no system for evaluating the performance of instructors, so decisions about reappointment were often arbitrary, sometimes to the detriment of the instructor, sometimes of her students.

I spent time and energy over some dozen years pressing for a regularization of the terms on which instructors served. One motive was fairness. Another was quality of instruction. With several colleagues, especially my close friends John Fischer and Panthea Reid, I convinced the English Department faculty, and then our department convinced the university to institute what we called the career instructorship. It worked this way: Before an instructor was hired for a third consecutive year, he/she would indicate whether he/she wished to be considered for a career instructorship. If so, during the third year, there was a methodical evaluation of her/his teaching by a committee, and the committee would then make a report to the tenured faculty, with whom the final decision resided. Those who were approved were given to understand that their annual contracts as full-time teachers would be renewed automatically for as long as they wished to stay on.

The result was that LSU had a more uniformly qualified corps of instructors, and they were more integrated into the life of their departments. They enjoyed respect, livable salaries, benefits, and job security. In a large number of other universities nationwide, that was not the case. Indeed, to its shame, higher education was one of the first sectors of our economy to develop a part-time, poorly paid, unbenefited, and insecure workforce. When I went back to academic life in 1990, after spending the previous three years as executive director of a large peace organization in northern New Jersey, I spent my first year in Houston as an instructor at the University of Houston. I was allowed to teach half time and was paid $8,000 for the academic year. The community colleges in the area were paying even less. I'm proud that at LSU, we did so much better.

I didn't regard the faculty as the most pressing challenge when it came to racial justice in campus employment. I knew from the start that the pool of Black PhDs was small and they would get jobs. It was staff that concerned me. There were more than two thousand jobs on campus requiring education and skills well within the compass of local Blacks—clerical work, landscape and building maintenance, food service, etc.—but I was observing no Blacks in positions other than the most menial. So, long before I got involved in faculty hiring, I focused there.

By 1967, the LSU chapter of AAUP had become a major forum of debate over institutional changes. Before, its membership had been small, made up of people concerned with the academic freedom of faculty members, which wasn't an endemic problem at LSU. But when the chapter began considering issues like the students' rights of free speech and assembly, conservative faculty joined as well. In the late sixties, the monthly meetings would attract fifty to one hundred attendees. One of the most contested issues was the two years of compulsory ROTC. In 1968, the AAUP Chapter recommended that it be abolished. After the upper administration became persuaded that the program was a flash point for student unrest, it presented a proposal to abolish it to the Faculty Council (the faculty gathered in plenary session) in October, and the Council approved. On May 26, 1969, the LSU Board of Supervisors made it official. Ours was one of the very last universities in the country to end compulsory ROTC.[9]

It was on my initiative that in early 1968, the chapter launched an investigation into racial bias in staff hiring. Five of us volunteered to do the work. Robert Pascal, a highly respected professor of law, chaired our committee, which proved a major asset. Largely thanks to Bob, I suspect, we got good cooperation from the Chancellor, the Comptroller, and the University Personnel Officer, who supplied us with a complete list of staff by positions and race. It displayed a color line as rigid as could be found in any sector of the economy. Blacks were concentrated in the most menial jobs—cooks, food servers, custodial workers, and groundskeepers. There were few Blacks in better-paid jobs like secretaries or carpenters or nurses. For example, 208 of 209 steno clerks II were White, as were 112 of the 113 typist clerks II. Further, with the exception of Custodial Services, few Blacks occupied supervisory positions.

The positions had differing classifications. About 250 were non-classified or unclassified. Only six Blacks held such jobs. The remaining 1814 positions were state civil service classified. The playing field for applicants for those jobs should have been level. That's because, under pressure, the Louisiana Department of State Civil Service had instituted tests for each position appropriate to the position (not general "intelligence" tests). The mandated procedure for filling a vacant position was for the agency (in this case, LSU) to send a request for applicants to State Civil Service.

In response, that office would send back to the agency the names and resumés of the three top test scorers currently registered with its office. Often, there were Blacks in the applicant pools, but departments and offices at LSU had found ways to frustrate that system. The most common was to fill the position on an interim basis and after six months convert the interim employee to a permanent status, which was allowed under Civil Service rules. As far as promotion went, there were no procedures in place to guard against racial bias.

As part of its work, the committee sent questionnaires both to faculty and staff to determine their attitudes toward working with Black staff, including having a Black supervisor. There were some procedural flaws in the way the questionnaires were distributed and retrieved. Still, we reliably discovered that faculty were overwhelmingly favorable or indifferent. The margin was smaller among the staff responses: 266 favorable or indifferent, 180 opposed. But only forty respondents said they would resign, and sixty-two said they would seek transfer to another department. The committee could thus report that, in addition to change being "demanded by social justice and eventually unavoidable," it "would not meet with such resistance as to render the move…administratively difficult."

Pascal pulled together all the information we had gathered into a beautifully organized report with recommendations for change. We presented it to the AAUP chapter, which had authorized the investigation. To my distress, those present at the meeting voted not to release the report to the media. It was released, along with its recommendations, to the university administration and constituted on-going pressure for remediation. Along with whatever good will existed at that level, the report constituted incontrovertible evidence that could be used by individuals complaining to the US Equal Employment Opportunity Commission. It didn't take long for the fruits of our work to manifest themselves. It soon became commonplace to see Black clerical workers when one walked into campus offices.

*****

In February 1976, Vice Chancellor for Student Affairs James W. Reddoch spoke at the Tenth Annual Alumni Leadership Workshop. He said, "The courts have ruled that the students' relationship with the institution has changed, and the relationship is now citizen-institutions." Actually, he meant that a series of court decisions on specific issues—he mentioned due process in suspensions, no prior approval of demonstrations, no prior censorship of student publications, and no regulation of personal appearance except for health reasons—"have created a framework in which universities must operate." He went on to say that LSU was "moving toward a system of equality in male and female housing regulations… They won't be exactly the same, but they'll be so close that there'll be no grounds for accusations of discrimination."

What the students' relationship with the institution had changed from by 1976 was *in loco parentis*—the assumption that undergraduates still needed parental guidance, which the college or university provided in place of their familial parents. That relationship implied that on campus, students didn't have many of the rights of citizens even if they had attained the age of legal majority. A corollary was that if students committed crimes on campus (such as theft from the bookstore) or off-campus got into trouble short of major felonies, it was common for local law enforcement to allow campus administrators to handle the matters as student disciplinary cases.

It was their lack of rights on campus that prompted student unrest across the nation. Like all of America's marginalized groups, they took their inspiration from the Civil Rights Movement. The connection was explicit in one of the earliest and certainly the most publicized student agitation—the Free Speech Movement at University of California-Berkley, which broke out in the fall, 1964. Some of its leaders had traveled with the Freedom Riders and had worked to register Blacks in Mississippi that summer. What triggered the outbreak on October 1 was when former graduate student Jack Weinberg was sitting at a CORE (Congress of Racial Equality) table and refused to show his identification to the campus police. When he was arrested, students surrounded the police car in which he was to be transported for booking. Over the ensuing thirty-two hours, as many as three thousand students prevented the car from leaving.

By 1966, even students in parts of the country historically quiescent were being drawn into the public forum by issues close to home—principally the Civil Rights Movement and the Vietnam War. But at LSU, as elsewhere, the public forum was narrowly circumscribed. There was a Free Speech Alley outside the student center that was open for two hours once a week. No other outdoor gatherings for the voicing of opinions were allowed unless permission was sought and granted by the administration. Nor was tabling or the distribution of materials except for approved flyers tacked on bulletin boards. Even materials hung on dorm room walls were subject to censorship.

Given a growing body of federal jurisprudence voiding such restrictions on First Amendment exercise (developments that the administration and its legal counsel followed closely), I was able to strengthen student demands for change with the threat of litigation.[10] As a consequence, those restrictions were the first set of student grievances to be redressed. For example, the restriction on unauthorized student gatherings was lifted during the 1968–1969 academic year.[11] Also, it wasn't a long struggle to build due process into student suspensions and to end efforts to regulate hair length and types of clothing in classrooms.[12] By 1970, there was an Office of the Ombudsman to hear student grievances, and by 1971, there was a student bill of rights.

Reform of other aspects of *in loco parentis* was slower. Rules governing women's dorm life was one, as can be inferred from Vice Chancellor Reddoch's remarks quoted above. Residents had to be back in the women's dorms by 10:00 p.m. on school nights, two hours before the library closed, in contrast to the midnight curfew for the men's dorms. There were nightly room checks. On weekends, the women had to sign out, indicating where they intended to go and when they would return, and the logs were kept on file permanently. Failure to return on time could result in grounding. There were even written personality profiles. As for male visitation, there was none allowed in the rooms.

All these restrictions stemmed from a tradition of protecting women, especially from sexual relations. I remember a debate in the Faculty Council about relaxing the restrictions. A male defended the status quo by saying that women are vulnerable to assault after 10:00 p.m. Nancy Heims from the Architecture School, one of the small number of women then in tenured faculty positions, replied by pointing out that since males were the perpetrators of such assaults, it was only proper to require them, not the women, to be in their dorms by 10:00 p.m. That wasn't going to happen.

There was a story, perhaps apocryphal, told of Mary Margaret Jameson, who became Dean of Women in 1966 after having served in that capacity at Mississippi State College for Women. Jameson had been born and raised in South Carolina and remained single all her life. She was immersed in the culture of Southern femininity. Supposedly she would meet with groups of incoming freshman women and ask them to pass from hand to hand a white magnolia blossom, which bruises quite easily. At the end of its rounds, the petals had become discolored, a concrete metaphor for women's fate in the hands of men.

Federal law and jurisprudence were considerably slower to support women's claims to equality than they were in other areas of civil rights and liberties, so we had less external leverage for change. In connection with a suit we filed on March 6, 1970, 1,200 women rallied that day seeking a volunteer rather than a mandatory curfew, the end to nightly room checks, and no permanent filing of sign-out cards. The suit also asked for an end to mandatory dorm living and meal plans[13] and the personality profiles. Federal District Judge E. Gordon West dismissed the suit, and we didn't pursue it further. So relaxations of the restrictions were voluntary concessions over time by the university. The first I remember was an end to the curfew and sign-out system for women whose parents or legal guardians gave signed permission.

Still another student right that needed defending was the right to vote. On July 1, 1971, the Twenty-sixth Amendment to the US Constitution took effect, enfranchising any citizen eighteen or older. Mildred Bankston, the parish Registrar of Voters, was willing to register students who lived off campus if they met state residency requirements but not students living on campus. Those students could request mail ballots from their hometowns, but the inconvenience discouraged participation in elections. In November, we sued Bankston to end the discrimination, which she subsequently did.

Students weren't interested in shedding the protection *in loco parentis* gave them from prosecution for crimes they committed on campus and, in some cases, off campus. But I was. The university campus as a space beyond the jurisdiction of civil authorities was a legal tradition going back as far as the earliest medieval universities. It created town-gown tensions then, and it was still creating them during my early years at LSU. That non-students would face fines or jail time for stealing at the university bookstore, for example, but students would face only academic discipline seemed an indefensible double standard. Acting as president of the state ACLU, in March 1971, I sent the chancellor a letter requesting that all alleged student crimes be turned over to the district attorney's office for investigation and possible prosecution and that the university limit its disciplinary authority to infractions of its own rules.

The university conceded jurisdiction in January of the following year. The primary impetus for change was reaction to its handling of an assault case by a varsity football player named Arthur Cantrelle. He had gotten into a fight off campus, and the arresting officers booked him for assault. The university persuaded the civil authorities (probably District Attorney Sargent Pitcher, who was a member of the LSU Board of Supervisors at the time) to turn the matter over to the LSU Athletic Department. But the incident attracted a good bit of public attention, and in a break with tradition, the university reversed itself. It returned the Cantrelle case to civil authority and announced that it would no longer handle criminal matters.

By August 1972, when I left town to begin a sabbatical year, those campus issues that had consumed a significant amount of my time and energy had been resolved satisfactorily or were in the process of resolution. And not coincidentally, LSU was on its way to becoming a more distinguished academic institution than it had been when I arrived seven years before. That change was yet another manifestation of the broad transition from a closed to an open society in the Deep South.

What hadn't been resolved, however, was when and how the Vietnam War would end.

*****

I can't pinpoint one experience that changed my attitude toward race relations. Everything I had absorbed growing up in New Orleans before the Civil Rights Movement and then watching the movement unfold, primarily from New England when I was in college and graduate school, led to my commitment to work for racial justice when I returned to Louisiana in 1965. Regarding our war in Vietnam, however, I remember precisely what changed my mind from uncritical acceptance of our government's justification for it to unwavering opposition. It was a Jules Feiffer cartoon in the *Village Voice*. I came across it in 1964, as I recall.

Here's how the cartoon went. There was a group of reporters listening to someone speaking outside the frame. For several frames, they heard statements like "There was no trouble in the South until outside agitators stirred it up," statements calculated to induce readers to assume that the speaker was someone like George Wallace. But then, in the last frame, the reporters responded, "Thank you for your thoughts on Vietnam, Mr. President." I knew I had my head straight about Jim Crow. Feiffer had shocked me into realizing that it was all wrong about the war.

During my first two years in Baton Rouge, I can recollect no organized events relating to the war except for a talk I gave to a fairly small audience at LSU about the way war constricts civil liberties. That quiescence wasn't surprising. In addition to its tradition of discouraging public debate and dissenting opinions, the South was the most militaristic section of the nation. Louisiana had major military installations, including Barksdale Air Force Base outside Shreveport, the Naval Support Activity complex on the river in New Orleans, and Fort Polk, a large infantry base in west central Louisiana. During the war, more soldiers were shipped to Vietnam from Fort Polk than from any other American training base because its heat and humidity and the jungle-like vegetation on part of its ten thousand acres approximated conditions in southeast Asia.

Johnson's rapid troop buildup had started right after his 1964 election, violating his campaign pledge that he would never send "American boys" to do what "Asian boys" should do for themselves. At the beginning of 1965, there were about 184,000 US troops there. After a year, there were 385,000. The numbers kept growing until they peaked at 536,000 in 1968. Because LSU students had 2S deferments, the intensified draft didn't threaten them right away. But year by year, it loomed larger and doubts about the legitimacy of our involvement began to grow, although there was no discernible activity beyond the campus. By fall 1967, at the event I recounted in Chapter 2, the antiwar remarks by Socialist Worker vice-presidential candidate Paul Boutelle were enthusiastically received by about 200 students.

Still, local sentiment overwhelmingly favored the war. Several months after the Tet offensive, launched on January 30, 1968, had cast general doubt on a US victory, including doubt by Johnson himself, General William Westmoreland, commander of US forces in Vietnam, was invited to speak on campus. A large crowd of students and faculty attended, and little skepticism was expressed when he asserted that Tet had finished the Viet Cong and all we had to do was stay the course. That year, one of the network-affiliated TV stations in Baton Rouge put together a panel on the war and invited me to participate. Another panel member was on the College of Agriculture faculty and fervently supported the war. After I spoke against it, the moderator asked whether my views were representative of the faculty. My colleague immediately responded with an emphatic "no." He was probably right.[14]

In 1969, after the apocalyptic events of the preceding year, the change that had swept over much of the country was manifesting itself locally. Students were trying to avoid the draft. Ben Shieber, a law professor, was doing draft counseling. We had a rally at the main post office, the first antiwar event off campus I can recall. Leonard Weinglass, one of the attorneys for the Chicago 8, whose prosecution arose from the police riot at the Democratic National Convention the previous August, spoke on campus to a large crowd and was well received. But the culminating event was our participation in the Moratorium to End the War in Vietnam, held worldwide on October 15. There was vigorous debate about whether the university should permit faculty to cancel their classes. I wrote a letter in the campus newspaper explaining why we had an obligation to our students to do so. Ultimately, each of us used our own judgment without repercussions. A sound stage was erected on the Parade Ground. About one thousand people turned up, the largest demonstration held during my twenty-two years at LSU. I was one of the speakers.

There was a second Moratorium day scheduled the following month, but no activities were planned on campus. I went out to a shopping center and distributed leaflets outside of one of its entrances. A security guard asked me to leave, and when I refused, he called the police and I was arrested. Encouraged by a recent Supreme Court ruling, I had hoped to assert in court that shopping centers, as quasi-public spaces, were open to First Amendment exercise.

Instead of being booked and printed, however, I was taken to the office of a police lieutenant. After a few minutes of confusion, I realized that his concern was that my intention was to make the police look bad. After I assured him it wasn't, he brought out a form releasing the department from liability, which I signed. I was then free to leave. As it turned out, that was fortunate. In the ensuing years, the jurisprudence on free speech at shopping centers went the wrong way.[15]

The last major event in connection with the war that I recall was a gathering on campus in response to the fatal shootings of four Kent State students by the Ohio National Guard. There was no debate about the war. Everyone present was unified in grief.

Because there seemed to be no end to our mass murder in Vietnam, I left for sabbatical in August 1972 with a heavy heart. Living outside Santa Cruz, California, I largely withdrew from public life for the only time in my adult life before or since. My wife and I did travel with our three young children to San Francisco to participate in a march protesting the Christmas bombing of Hanoi and Haiphong. That intense assault, named Operation Linebacker II, lasted twelve days. B52s dropped some fifteen thousand tons of explosives, the largest B52 strikes ever. The devastation was horrific. It was our government's last effort to secure what Nixon called "peace with honor."

---

[1] The per-student funding formulas used to allocate state monies to public universities typically rewarded graduate student headcounts, and especially doctoral headcounts, at much higher rates than undergraduate headcounts. In

addition, departments like English, Mathematics, and Foreign Languages, which had to keep their introductory class sizes fairly small, depended heavily on the cheap labor of graduate teaching assistants. So universities were eager to establish and/or expand graduate programs during the big expansion of college-going, and reluctant to reduce admissions to those programs regardless of an academic job market that was able to absorb fewer and fewer of their graduates as the 1970s progressed.

2   One consequence was that students couldn't major in a subject area, such as mathematics, and still get enough education course credits to be certified. While it is perhaps appropriate for those teaching at the elementary school level to major in education, certainly for high school teaching and arguably for middle school as well, knowledge of the subject matter of the courses they teach is the primary qualification.

3   The entrenched tenures of most of its administrators was a major obstacle to LSU's progress both educationally and culturally. Deans served indefinite terms at the pleasure of the president, and many departments were run by "heads," not chairs, serving indefinitely at the pleasure of their deans. The head of my department (English) retired in 1973 after more than three decades in office. He was fairly liberal in political and social outlook, which was fortunate for me, but disinterested in raising the academic quality of the faculty. Some heads were worse, such as St. John Chilton, head of the Department of Botany and Plant Pathology, about whom I wrote in Chapter 1. The phasing out of appointments of deans and department heads for unfixed terms coincided with, and contributed significantly to, the university's academic advancement. The same terms of administrative tenure obtained in the other state colleges and universities, only to a worse degree. Faculties there had less say over

academic life than we did at LSU. Needless to say, academic distinction was scarce.

4   Southern University ran an identical lab school, which was a main reason that the Black educational establishment centered at Southern was not interested in supporting meaningful racial integration of the parish public schools (see Chapter 6).

5   The law school, part of LSU in Baton Rouge, integrated earlier. Ernest "Dutch" Morial, who later was to become the first Black mayor of New Orleans (1978–1986), graduated in 1954. The reason state professional schools often were desegregated by court order before *Brown v. Board* of *Education* (1954) was that if a state didn't provide for a separate institution for Blacks, the state couldn't claim it was providing separate but equal facilities, and "separate but equal" was the law of the land before *Brown*.

An interesting footnote to the desegregation of LSU's undergraduate programs was that in 1953, a Black student named Alexander Pierre Tureaud Jr. enrolled. His admission was pursuant to a temporary court injunction obtained by his father, A. P. Tureaud Sr., the leading civil rights attorney in Louisiana during the 1950s and into the 1960s. The son, A. P. Jr., endured two months of ostracism and harassment before the injunction was lifted and he was expelled by court order. He then enrolled at, and later graduated from, Xavier University, a fine historically Black Catholic university in New Orleans. On May 20, 2011, LSU awarded Tureaud an honorary doctorate. He said in an interview with the *Louisiana Weekly* that his father "really did not recruit me. I volunteered to go because I felt that it was a good school for the money." But he added, "I endured more than I thought. I made a mistake, it wasn't what I wanted. College was supposed to be the best time of my life. I didn't go there to be a martyr, although I know I've set a precedent in terms of legal action." For more on A. P. Tureaud Sr., see *A More Noble Cause* by Rachel Emanuel, published in 2011 by the LSU Press.

[6] After graduation, Pourciau held various positions in government, including working for US Senator Russell Long and New Orleans Mayor Ernest N. Morial. He was working for State Attorney General Billy Guste in 1984 when I ran for Congress in the Sixth District. At the start of my campaign, Kerry was my "dresser"; he took me shopping for appropriate clothes. At his urging, I spent more on a suit and a sport coat than I had spent before or since. Kerry died in 1994, much too young. In 2015 the LSU Office of Diversity instituted the Black Male Leadership Initiative/Kerry Pourciau and Kirk Bennett Leadership Award. Bennett was the second Black to become SGA president.

An earlier indication of the attitude of LSU's White students toward Blacks occurred the morning after Martin Luther King's assassination on April 4, 1968. A large number gathered around the flag pole on the Parade Ground, a big roughly oval-shaped grassy area so named because the ROTC instructors used to parade their students on it when the program was compulsory (see note 9 below and its associated text above). The students were demanding that the flag be lowered to half-mast. There were no dissenters present. About an hour after the gathering started, the chancellor, Cecil "Pete" Taylor, arrived, explaining that he had been at the dentist. As I remember it, he hemmed and hawed for a time and tried to pass responsibility to the commander of the ROTC unit, which did raise and lower the flag daily. He soon realized, however, that he had to defuse an explosive situation, and on his instruction, the flag was lowered.

The last indication I'll cite is a finding by a study of racial discrimination in university employment that was conducted that same spring (discussed later in this chapter). While there was pervasive discrimination everywhere else, we found none in student employment.

[7] To avoid racial mixing on the field, between 1940 and 1970 LSU played few football teams outside the South. LSU, Ole Miss, and Georgia integrated their football teams in 1972, the last schools in the Southeastern Conference (SEC) to do so. About that same time, the basketball program was integrated. Especially in that sport, once change began, it progressed quickly. During the 1969–1970 basketball season, there were two Blacks among 120 SEC players. By 1975, they constituted 45 percent of the players.

[8] But by the later 1970s, after the job market had tightened so drastically even PhDs began to accept offers as instructors, hoping to publish some research and go out on the job market again in a stronger position.

[9] LSU had a long historical connection with the military. The legislation founding it in 1853 named it the Louisiana State Seminary of Learning & Military Academy, to be modeled after Virginia Military Institute. It opened in 1860 with then-Colonel William Tecumseh Sherman as superintendent, who is credited with nicknaming it the "Ole War Skule." It was reopened after the Civil War in Baton Rouge as Louisiana State University, an all-male school at which every student had to complete military training in the LSU Corps of Cadets. Sometime after the university became coed, male students were required to take only two years of ROTC (which entailed having their heads shaved upon matriculation). The year before the program was made voluntary, there were about three thousand males enrolled. The volunteer program, attracting only those who are pursuing commissions, enrolls a few hundred, both male and female.

[10] While not the first relevant case law, it was in its *Tinker v. Des Moines Independent Community School District* decision,

handed down on November 12, 1968, that the US Supreme Court memorably declared that students do not "shed their constitutional rights at the school house gate." Actually, the plaintiffs in *Tinker* were younger than college students. They were high school and junior high school students who wore black arm bands to school on December 16, 1965, to protest the war in Vietnam.

11 It took longer to compel the university to open the public areas of the campus to free exercise by anyone. As late as 1974, I had to challenge it to allow townspeople to distribute their publications. The judicial guideline is that public facilities are open to First Amendment exercise as long as it doesn't interfere with the primary purpose of the facility. Facilities where security is a consideration, such as prisons and military bases, are treated as exceptions. Also, a distinction can be made between commercial and political speech/literature. In 1982, I spent five days in jail educating the Baton Rouge postmaster on the law and his own agency's regulation. Years later, I had to court arrest to teach the same lesson to postmasters in Central Point and Phoenix, small cities in southern Oregon, where I now live. It's not unusual for public officials to be ignorant of the relevant laws and regulations governing their conduct.

12 However, the chancellor, by then Paul Murrill, did uphold the band director's dismissal from the program of a student whose hair he deemed was too long.

13 LSU was largely a residential campus. If students were from the area, they were permitted to live at home, and out-of-town students could apply for permission to live with a relative in the area. Married students could live in married student apartments or in town. Over time, there was general student pressure for off-campus living, but the university yielded to it only at a pace that didn't jeopardize its ability to

pay off with student housing fees the bonds it had issued to build new dorms when enrollments expanded rapidly in the sixties.

14 The unique nature of Louisiana law was responsible for government recruitment of LSU Law School faculty into the war effort, some of whom may otherwise have opposed it. Unlike the other forty-nine states, Louisiana civil law derived not from the English but the continental European Roman law tradition. The French had imposed their law in Vietnam during its colonial rule (1887–1954). After they were defeated and left, the United States tried to build a heretofore nonexistent separate nation in the southern half of the country. One aspect of the project was to construct a legal regime around the dictatorship we had installed. During much of the sixties, several law school professors whom I knew rather well were paid handsomely to help with that project. I was certain it would ultimately come to naught, but they believed in the worth of their work.

15 In *Amalgamated Food Employees Union v. Logan Valley Plaza, Inc.*, 391 US 308, 318 (1968), the court ruled that a labor union had a right to picket a store in a shopping center. Soon after, however, the court became more conservative thanks to Nixon's appointments, and it reversed itself on the issue. That didn't quite lay the issue to rest, however. While its 1980 decision in a case originating in California reiterated earlier rulings, in it the court said that such activity could be protected in California because the state Supreme Court had ruled that the California constitution guaranteed the right (*Pruneyard Shopping Ctr. v. Robins*, 447 US 74, 80). New Jersey subsequently followed California's lead. Beyond its relevance to the particular issue, the *Pruneyard* ruling was important in affirming that state constitutions could grant rights beyond those granted by the federal constitution.

# CHAPTER 5

## An Inexplicable Obsession

A Baton Rouge acquaintance of mine who grew up in a small Louisiana town shared with me the following experience from her childhood.

One evening, a well-dressed Black man whom she knew came to the door of her home. She greeted him then called to her father, "Mr. —— wants to talk with you." After the visitor had left, her father slapped her across the face. "You never call a Negro by his last name."

Most of us who grew up in that culture cannot point to so dramatic a tutorial in White supremacy and Black inferiority. We didn't need it. Simply to live there was to learn its fundamental rules.

We never saw Black people exercising authority over Whites and rarely saw them functioning as equals.[1] They were almost always subordinates—domestic servants, janitors, ditch diggers, street cleaners, golf caddies. In a large Southern city like New Orleans, which has two historically Black colleges (Dillard and Xavier), there were Black professionals, but we had little to no contact with them. This *de facto* arrangement was underscored by legal segregation of public facilities and the exclusion of Blacks from private facilities except as menial employees.

In a meaningful sense, there was less residential segregation in New Orleans when I was growing up than later, after school integration prompted massive White flight. Before that, there were many small Black neighborhoods check-by-jowl with White neighborhoods. We called the one that ran behind the houses on my street the "Back Lot." The demarcations were obvious, not only in the quality of the housing but also in the presence or absence of sidewalks, proper drainage, and street lighting. But people—especially kids—crossed the boundaries frequently.

Which leads to the larger point that for almost all Southern Whites, Blacks were part of our lives. They were familiar, not alien, and I never remember being afraid of a Black person, though God knows they had great reason to be afraid of Whites, especially the New Orleans police.[2]

For me, at least, that familiarity helped ease my re-acculturation when the social and legal circumstances that had schooled me to be a racist began to crumble. And to varying degrees, I think the same was true for large numbers of us. The Civil Rights Movement and the enormous changes it brought about gave us White captives of Southern culture a chance for freedom. My guess is that without realizing it or even desiring it, most of us made something of that chance. In large part, attitude follows behavior, so when our behavior had to alter, so did our mental state.

Did we cease being racists? Certainly not. Louisiana politics—and Southern politics generally—continues to be distorted by racism. And to this day, after decades of conscious as well as unconscious change, I occasionally find a racist thought pop into my mind in response to some external prompt. So when Whites of my generation in or from the South deny that they are expressing racist attitudes when I suggest they are, I give their claims no credence. We were dyed in the wool. The tint can fade to a faintness undetectable to others, but I fear we are never washed clean.

*****

Thus far, I've spoken only of our literally commonplace racism. There is another kind. Many may prefer to regard the difference between the two as a difference of degree, and I've no desire to argue the point. They may be right. But I wish to speak of it at some length because it puzzles me.

To my knowledge, I've personally known only one such racist, David Duke. He enrolled at LSU as a freshman in fall 1968. From the outset, he stridently proclaimed his Nazi sympathies, often holding forth at what was called Free Speech Alley next to the student union. Inevitably, his activities led him to seek my help in defending his civil liberties, which more than once were threatened with abridgment.[3]

Duke was bright, articulate, well-groomed, and polite. He invariably called me "Dr. Rothschild" and spoke to me respectfully. It was an extraordinary experience because all the time he was sitting a few feet away from me in my office, I was aware that if he had the power, he would send me to the gas chamber. Not because he disliked me—I had the sense that the opposite was true. It was simply that I was an ethnic

Jew, and my belonging to that group trumped all personal experience.

As I've tried to understand such a mind, my own extensive experience with racism has been an inadequate guide. Duke's racism seemed independent of the social system that had formed my bigotry. Nor could I discern a psychological origin. Unlike so many of the pathetic adherents of skinhead and militia groups I encounter in the pages of the Southern Poverty Law Center's *Intelligence Report*, Duke didn't strike me as propping up his self-esteem with a conviction of his racial superiority. He had a lot of personal gifts going for him. He could have made a place in the world for himself without espousing his ugly ideology. Indeed, in some meaningful ways, he has sacrificed a great deal to his Baal.

As far-fetched as it may seem, it was Cervantes's *Don Quixote* who provided me with what I considered an illuminating parallel. In the novel, people who've heard about Quixote's obsession with knight errantry often marvel at his behavior when they finally meet him. On every topic but one he speaks intelligently, often insightfully, drawing upon a clear-eyed knowledge of the world. But when the subject of knight errantry arises, his mental processes shift into an entirely different gear. He continues to speak articulately, and his disposition remains gentle even when he battles the foe. But he enters a different conceptual frame, one that is self-contained and immune to modification by any experiences he has, no matter how painful (and mostly they are painful).

My most publicized defense of Duke's civil liberties occurred in 1971. It was occasioned by his effort to rent a public high school auditorium to hold a meeting for a hate group he led. His application was denied. The denial violated the East Baton Rouge Parish School District's long-standing policy that allowed groups to use an auditorium for open-to-the-public events when the facility was available and a small fee to cover the extra utilities and janitorial expense was paid in advance.

On Duke's behalf, I requested time at a school board meeting to appeal the decision. It was granted. The school board met far from the LSU campus, and I always rode my bike to work. So on the afternoon of the scheduled meeting, one of his people drove him and me to it. Duke and I sat side-by-side in the back seat. Nothing happened on the ride, but I was uncomfortable. I felt I was on turf he controlled.

At the meeting, I argued to the school board that the policy couldn't be applied in a manner that discriminated based on the ideology of the applicant or the views that would be expressed at the event. The school board could choose to end its use policy, but as long as it existed, it had to be applied in a politically neutral way. I pointed to federal court decisions that mandated neutrality. Duke then spoke. He began by saying he never thought the day would come when he'd be defending civil liberties.

His declaration was just one of that day's ironies. Another was that the school board members were still all White, and if their actions in response to the 1970 federal court order to create a racially unitary school district were an indication, they were racist. Still another was that in 1966, a Klan meeting had been held in a school auditorium. And then there was the relatively striking fact that I was an ethnic Jew, which I mentioned in my presentation.

The sole spokesperson supporting the denial of use was a Jewish man from one of the two synagogues in town. I hadn't met him before. He argued that the school board shouldn't abet the spread of hatred. His was a reasonable position, but one that I—and the ACLU—regarded as wrong both in principle and as a strategy for protecting minorities like Jews from persecution.[4] In the next day's *Morning Advocate*, the story included side-by-side photographs of him, Duke, and me.

The school board overruled the administrative decision denying Duke the permit. Unfortunately, some ignorant official from the US Department of Health, Education, and Welfare (HEW) threatened the school district with loss of federal funds if it granted Duke's application. Understandably, the school board reversed itself. We had to seek redress in court. When we did, HEW backed out, leaving the school board alone to defend itself. Eventually, we won in the Fifth U.S. Circuit Court of Appeals, which was accustomed to striking down selectively applied rules.

Duke graduated from LSU in 1974, and I didn't see him again for years. But he was frequently in the news, and I followed his efforts to win high political office in Louisiana and even the US presidency. The farthest he got was one four-year term in the Louisiana House of Representatives, where he had little impact. His main effort, a bill requiring recipients of state and federal welfare benefits to undergo drug testing, didn't pass.

In 1991, however, Duke impacted my personal life in an odd way.

My second wife, to whom I was then married, worked for eight years for the State of Louisiana. When we moved to New Jersey in 1987, she left her retirement contributions in the system, thinking that if we returned to Louisiana, she would need to work as a state employee only two more years to get vested. I thought she could do better if she took her money out of the system, which was paying her no interest on it, and establish an IRA. I pointed out that she could make a great deal more as a legal secretary, which she became after our move, than the state would pay her as a clerical worker. My reasoning didn't persuade her, and I realized that what was really at stake wasn't the money but her emotional tie to Louisiana.

A death in her family required us to move back South in 1990, but we moved to Houston because the job prospects were better there and it was as close as Baton Rouge to the people we needed to care for. The next year, the Governor's Race from Hell took place in Louisiana. David Duke and former three-time governor Edwin Edwards got into the run-off. That was when the justly famous bumper sticker could be seen in New Orleans: "Vote for the crook; it's important."

Duke polled just under 40 percent of the total vote, but he won about 55 percent of the White vote. Right afterward, my wife told me she was withdrawing her money from the retirement system. It was her declaration of independence from her native state.

The 1991 gubernatorial election epitomized politics in the South since the 1970s in that when Democrats win statewide, it's almost always with a minority of White votes and a huge majority of Black votes. That reality prevented Robert Bork from becoming a US Supreme Court Justice.

When Ronald Reagan nominated Bork in 1987, he anticipated opposition from Democratic senators from outside the South. What he didn't anticipate was that they would be joined by Democratic senators from the former Confederate states. Only one, Hollings from South Carolina, voted yes. Thirteen Southern senators, including both from Louisiana, voted no. The story I heard was that J. Bennett Johnston, Louisiana's senior senator, called his colleagues together and told them they were going to vote against Bork's confirmation for the same reason he was—that they all were in office by virtue of Black votes, and Black leaders had made Bork's confirmation a bellwether vote.

The contest between Duke and Edwards also epitomized Louisiana politics, which so often has pitted a corrupt but mildly progressive Democrat against a relatively honest but politically conservative, if not reactionary, Republican.

Edwards was the most cynical person I ever knew. His working assumption was that everyone was for sale, and I guess that his decades of experience in Louisiana politics did little to shake that assumption. Like Iago in *Othello*, Edwards had the self-flattering but perverse idea that because he was candid about being corrupt, he was more honest than most of us. His shamelessness struck a chord among many Louisiana voters, who will tell you that all politicians are corrupt and won't believe that politics in other states are more decent than theirs.

Cynicism is the dominant key of Louisiana politics, and for a quarter century, Edwards was its maestro. My sister told me her Edwards story. She and her husband were in a Las Vegas casino. One of their New York friends who was with them in Las Vegas asked, "What's the salary of the governor of Louisiana?" They made an educated guess and asked him why he wished to know. "Because I just watched your governor lose a year's salary at the craps table."

Edwards was unapologetic about his highly publicized gambling, at times using tongue-in-cheek aliases like T. Wong and E. Lee. There's an old section of Baton Rouge called Spanish Town not far from the Governor's Mansion that annually had a Mardi Gras celebration. The year Edwards's gambling aliases made the papers, some of my friends dressed in Chinese costumes and named their parade float "Louisiana craps out."

Vastly different though Edwards and Duke were, they shared an addiction to gambling. And it later landed both of them in federal prison, Duke for a year-and-a-half for soliciting campaign funds with which he then gambled and Edwards for more than eight years for various crimes relating to casino licenses as well as a private juvenile prison in Louisiana. After his release, Edwards tried to win a Congressional seat but failed. Duke resumed his calling as a propagandist for racism and anti-Semitism, and in 2016, he too made what I presume will be his last bid for public office. He ran for US senator in Louisiana and garnered just over 3 percent of the votes.[5]

The last time I saw Duke was sometime in the 1990s at a Mexican restaurant in Baton Rouge. I had come over from Houston to visit two of my children and their kids. As we were walking to our table, I heard a voice call out, "Dr. Rothschild." I turned and there was Duke, standing with his hand extended toward me. After briefly hesitating, I shook it and walked on.

Ever since, I've been unable to decide whether I should have done that.

---

[1] In 1957, the summer after I graduated from high school, I worked on a construction job. Almost every craft union was segregated by race. Plumbers, carpenters, electricians, and equipment operators were all White. Laborers and hod carriers were all Black. The masons, however, were an integrated union. I never learned the historical circumstances that created so striking an exception to the rule.

[2] The children of Joseph Giarrusso, longtime chief of the New Orleans Police Department, were my father's patients. Dad told me that once, when he made a house call to attend one of the children, Giarrusso told him that the police had to keep the Black population in a state of constant intimidation or they would run wild.

[3] In addition to efforts to keep Duke from distributing literature on campus, in 1970, initially, he was not allowed to register for the advanced ROTC program. Under our pressure, he was admitted but told it was unlikely he would be commissioned.

[4] The same issues arose in a far more publicized case in 1976, when the city of Skokie, Illinois, passed three highly restrictive parade and public assembly ordinances to deny a Nazi group from Chicago a permit to march through town in their uniforms. While similar ordinances had been routinely passed by Southern towns as a way to frustrate Civil Rights marches, what seemed to attract the national media in the Skokie case was that more than half the town's population was Jewish and some were Holocaust survivors. The ACLU successfully challenged the ordinance on constitutional grounds. The attorney was Jewish.

[5] In Spike Lee's 2018 film *BlacKkKlansman*, Duke is a prominent character. And when the film ends with some documentary

footage from the 2017 alt-right rally in Charlottesville, he appears in proper person excitedly proclaiming the new era for White supremacists that Trump's presidency has supposedly inaugurated. That promise was a pipe dream for Duke, and if Lee meant to alarm us about a return to the early 1970s, when the events of his film took place, he was a poor observer of the political scene. As evidence, I cite the difference between Duke's showing at the polls in 1991 and in 2016. I also note that during Trump's presidency, more Confederate monuments were removed than in all preceding presidencies combined, including the prominently placed statue of Robert E. Lee atop a tall column in Lee Circle at the foot of St. Charles Avenue in New Orleans. As I wrote in the preface to this book, I don't want to dissuade anyone from deep engagement in efforts to overcome continuing racial injustice, but the struggles and sacrifices of the times I'm recalling were not in vain.

# CHAPTER 6

# Integrating Baton Rouge Schools

It was a foregone conclusion that racial integration of the public schools in Orleans Parish would fail miserably. I didn't think that was true of the public schools in East Baton Rouge Parish when their integration began in February, 1970.[1] But foregone or not, the conclusion there was equally disastrous.

New Orleans had never made a commitment to good public education. That was because the most influential people, both White and Black, sent their children to private schools. Indeed, the private school to which a family sent its children was a key indicator of its position in the city's elaborately differentiated social hierarchies. When two people of my generation meet for the first time and discover that they both grew up in New Orleans, they are likely to ask each other which high school they attended. It's a rather reliable social marker.

Also, there was an extensive Catholic school system in New Orleans, which meant that those it served had little commitment to public schools. Indeed, beginning in the 1970s, when a dearth of religious vocations required the schools to pay larger faculty salaries than when much of the instruction was done by nuns, the archdiocese became competitive at the state legislature for education dollars in the form of vouchers.[2]

Lack of support for public schools expressed itself in a long-standing unwillingness to levy property taxes at a rate to fund quality, plus a more general disinterest by those best positioned to take responsibility. And all this was before racial integration. Once that happened, there was major White flight of those unable to afford private schooling. They moved into neighboring Jefferson Parish, where the percentage of Black residents was much lower than in Orleans Parish. Interstate Highway 10, plus an expanded downtown bridge over the Mississippi to the portion of Jefferson Parish on the west bank of the river, made it relatively easy for people to live outside New Orleans yet work in it (an unhappy collusion of public policy and private bigotry not unique to New Orleans).

With a shrunken property tax base, poor school board leadership, and a legacy of separate but unequal Black educational achievement, the New Orleans public school system failed. The physical plants were so deteriorated and the students so low performing that when Hurricane Katrina struck the city on August 29, 2005, and damaged or destroyed 100 of the 128 schools, it was a blessing. With intervention from the state, a vast reconfiguration has occurred—93 percent of students currently attend public charter schools—and student performance is already exceeding pre-Katrina levels. Some of the specialized schools have significant racial diversity.

Among the several reasons I wasn't tempted to return to New Orleans after finishing my graduate work was that I didn't want to send my children to private schools, although I had attended one from kindergarten through high school. Aside from the expense, I didn't wish to be caught up in the social stratification endemic to the city. In Baton Rouge, we could send our children to public schools, which we did.

First, they attended Walnut Hills Elementary, about three miles east of the LSU campus on S. Acadian Throughway near Hundred Oaks. If there were any Black students or faculty when our first child enrolled in 1967, they were too few to remember now. Close to the school and our home was a fairly small all-Black neighborhood called Valley Park, surrounded by White neighborhoods. Its residents attended an elementary and a middle school located in Valley Park.

In the summer of 1969, the principal of Walnut Hills called a parents' meeting, which I attended. Its focus hadn't been announced in advance. When it began, she explained that the next year, there would be court-ordered integration of the school's faculty and students. Valley Park Elementary was to be closed and its students assigned to Walnut Hills. She regarded this development as a blow. So although she knew racial integration was inevitable, she wanted help in convincing the school board to assign more of the Black students to Westdale Elementary, another all-White school on the far side of Valley Park. A number of parents agreed with that plan. Others said they would take their children out of the school. I expressed my disappointment in the resistance to integration and my confidence that a racially integrated Walnut Hills would remain a fine school.

The principal's hope wasn't realized. She resigned. In the first semester of the 1970 school year, faculty were assigned to schools across East Baton Rouge Parish in roughly a 2:1 White-to-Black ratio, echoing the racial makeup of its population. However, the court didn't treat the district as similarly unitary for student assignment (a crucial point to which I'll soon return). So it was that Walnut Hills had a 50-50 student makeup the first year. The enrollment later rose to 60 percent Black then leveled out and soon returned to approximately 50-50. That ratio obtained at least through the 1975 school year, the last year any of our children were of elementary school age. The educational quality, as far as we could discern, didn't erode.

Walnut Hills was a success story. The precondition of its success was the unchanging residential pattern in the area from which its students were drawn. Housing in Valley Park was low income; housing in the adjacent areas was largely unaffordable to Black people. So there was no panicked selling in the White neighborhoods. The home-owners who resisted school integration didn't move; they just sent their children to private schools. And as it became known that Walnut Hills was still a strong learning environment, some of those parents reenrolled their kids.

That was the precondition. A condition of success was that the White students were from well-educated families, which is the best predictor of school success. Another condition was that parents took a strong interest in the school, supporting its principal and teachers in various ways. My children's mother became Walnut Hills's half-time art teacher at no pay; thus, it became the only elementary school in the district with an art program. Also, the new principal was gifted and committed to making integration succeed. The integrated faculty got along well. An unusual and extraordinary bright spot was that the school board chose to house at Walnut Hills its program for students who were both blind and deaf. The teacher in charge enlisted regular students to help his students. All these factors contributed to a strong school morale.

Such successes were few. Failure was almost guaranteed by the refusal of the court to treat the school district as unitary in regard to student as well as faculty assignment. The local NAACP chapter, which in 1968 had become the main plaintiff in *Davis v. East Baton Rouge School Board*, had asked the federal district court to do so.[3] Three forces frustrated that outcome.

One was the plan itself, developed after the Fifth Circuit Court of Appeals declared that the "freedom of choice" plan, approved by Federal District Judge E. Gordon West[4] in 1963, had achieved no meaningful integration, only token desegregation. Under a new mandate, the parish school board had eliminated the freedom-of-choice provision and formed a biracial committee to help develop a new plan. That plan was based on new neighborhood student attendance zones and voluntary majority-to-minority transfer provisions, which allowed any student attending a school where his or her race was the majority to transfer to a school where his or her race was the minority. But most Blacks at that time resided in three large areas of the city, referred to as Scotlandville, Eden Park, and South Baton Rouge,[5] not in relatively small enclaves like Valley Park. So they were clustered into neighborhood attendance zones, and few parents were inclined to send their children to majority White schools.

There was a large historically blue-collar White residential area commonly called North Baton Rouge, bounded on the west by the Exxon refinery and other petrochemical plants along the river where many of the residents worked and on the east by Airline Highway. North and south, it was bounded by two of the three large Black areas, so the new neighborhood attendance zoning meant that some of the schools there would be meaningfully integrated. The owners also were fearful of residential integration because the value of their properties was modest. So "For sale" signs sprouted like mushrooms throughout the area, and within two years, it had flipped. Whites fled southeast toward Ascension Parish and east toward Livingston Parish. The I-10 and I-12 arteries facilitated White flight. The commute to the plants became hellish—during rush hours traffic at the I-10/I-12 split remains a nightmare to this day—but it was a price Whites were willing to pay.

A second force working against successful integration was the school board, elected at large rather than from single member districts (see Chapter 8) and thus all White at that time. When it tried to terminate the position of librarian at Walnut Hills and a few other successfully integrated elementary schools (we thwarted that attempt), it seemed obvious to those of us committed to racial integration that segregation remained the board's primary objective.

Our major pushback came in 1974, when the board put before voters a ballot measure for a five-mill tax that would generate $18.5 million over five years for school construction and improvement. At public meetings, the board refused to give specifics about how it intended to use the proceeds. There was a strong suspicion that even though the school-age population wasn't expanding, most of the funds would be used to construct new schools to encourage White flight. A skilled activist named Jackie Ducote[6] helped create the Inner-City School Council, a coalition of Blacks and Whites whose children were attending integrated or all Black schools. The coalition opposed the tax, and on November 5, it was defeated. It sent a clear message. But our victory merely delayed what proved to be an unstoppable drive to defeat thorough-going and permanent integration.

The school board's handling of Baton Rouge High School was typical of its bad faith. Baton Rouge High was one of the two original White high schools in the city; the other was Istrouma. Given the patterns of residential settlement as the city's population grew, they became inner city schools, but in 1970, there were still large numbers of White families in their geographic districts. Istrouma was in blue-collar North Baton Rouge, and the White flight from that area, which I described above, doomed its chance of successful racial mixing. Not so Baton Rouge High. It drew White students from neighborhoods like mine as well as Black students from nearby all-Black neighborhoods.

My next-door neighbors, whose children were older than ours, had their two youngest enrolled there. That was an extraordinary act of faith on their part. The father was from Philadelphia, Mississippi, and was overtly racist. The mother was from Yazoo City, Mississippi, and though not overtly racist, like all of us, she had been acculturated to think segregation was the correct arrangement. Nevertheless, they accepted the arrangement without any complaint I ever heard them utter. But soon the school board began floating rumors that Baton Rouge High might be closed. The uncertainty continued for more than two years, and it broke the morale of the school. Enrollment fell. My oldest child was scheduled to enter her freshman year in the fall of 1976, and if the school closed, I had resolved to home school her rather than let her be assigned to an almost all-White suburban school, where we heard there was a significant drug problem. That didn't happen. In the spring the school board announced that Baton Rouge High would become a magnet school for academically strong students. So we did enroll my daughter and, in subsequent years, our two sons. The school was good, and it had a fairly sizable Black enrollment. Still, the school board could have chosen a different high school—not the only one that had been successfully integrated simply by drawing on students from within its own district—as one of the two magnet schools it established.

The magnet school scheme brings me to the third force working against successful integration, the Black educational establishment centered at Southern University. Southern is one of two historically Black public universities in Louisiana—the other is Grambling up in north Louisiana—and was at the time the largest Black university in the nation. Both of them had been important to the welfare of their people all during the Jim Crow years. And to the people in charge of those institutions, desegregation was a welcome change: no more humiliation in public.

But integration was something else. Their status and power came from running overwhelmingly Black schools.

Both universities were run as personal fiefdoms by the top administrators. When I joined the LSU faculty, Southern and Grambling had long been on the censure list of the American Association of University Professors for violations of its 1940 Statement of Principles on Academic Freedom and Tenure. The presidents worked hard to suppress student agitation during a period when protest was commonplace on US campuses. In 1967, the ACLU filed a suit against Ralph Waldo Emerson Jones, longtime president of Grambling, on behalf of some students he had expelled without any hearing for exercising their First Amendment rights of speech and assembly. And I learned that John Netterville, president of Southern, sent letters to the parents of all the students warning that if their children engaged in protests, their financial aid would be cut off.

The worst episode occurred on November 16, 1972, when Southern students were staging the latest in a series of protests to make the administration more responsive to their needs. Governor Edwin Edwards sent East Baton Rouge Sheriff Department deputies to campus. Tear gas was used, and a deputy fatally shot undergraduates Denver Smith and Leonard Brown. No one was ever charged in the shooting. Willie Jenkins, Brown's brother, said that when the families tried to get redress, "We didn't get help from Netterville or Governor Edwards. No lawyers would talk to us and the ones who did were ran out of town."[7] But the student union was renamed the Smith-Brown Memorial Union in February 1973, and years later, on March 31, 2017, the Southern

University System's academic affairs committee voted unanimously to award posthumous degrees to Smith and Brown.

A primary function of historically Black universities was to credential teachers and administrators for the segregated schools. During Jim Crow, Whites cared nothing about the quality of Southern or its graduates. With integration, that changed. Undoubtedly, for students of both races, the change was for the better, but it understandably put the Black educational establishment on the defensive. Its members successfully resisted integration of Southern with LSU,[8] and they succeeded in derailing any integration plan that would end their control of historically all-Black public schools in Baton Rouge. The local NAACP chapter, which sought the creation of a unitary system in regard to student assignments, was overmatched by the combination of the White school board and the Black educational establishment.

Two magnet schools were established as a way to induce qualified students to enroll voluntarily beyond their assigned districts. Baton Rouge High was one, McKinley the other. After I left the state, the school board added more magnet schools and programs. The impact was modest. By 2017, although the population of East Baton Rouge Parish was approximately 49 percent White and 46 percent Black, 71 percent of the 57,781 students in the parish public schools were Black and only 19 percent were White.[9]

The experience of West Feliciana Parish, which borders East Baton Rouge Parish on the north and extends along the river to the Mississippi border, suggests that failure wasn't inevitable. West Feliciana is small—only 15,625 residents according to the 2010 census. It had segregated schools, but after integration, there was only one school at each level. Thus, the system was unitary both for faculty and students. Some White families who could afford it pulled out their children and sent them to a private "Christian" academy across the state border. The large majority of students, however, went to the integrated public schools. Their racial makeup at all levels currently is about 58 percent White, 40 percent Black, and 2 percent Other. This is a higher ratio of Blacks to Whites than would have been the case in East Baton Rouge Parish in 1970 had a unitary system been implemented.

Two of my children raised their children in West Feliciana Parish and sent them to the public schools from elementary through high school. The four kids all got a good education. The graduation rate from West Feliciana High School is 82 percent, although 47 percent of the student body is classified as economically disadvantaged. Interestingly, the average college entrance exam score of the Black students is just about that of the White students. Nor were there racial tensions among the students. For many years, there were racially separate senior proms, but the students themselves put an end to that.

---

[1] I distinguish here between desegregation and integration. Desegregation, which began earlier, ended legally mandated one-race schools. It allowed Black children and their families who were brave enough to choose to cross the color line to enroll in previously all White schools. Integration ended this exclusive reliance on choice, which had done little to change the racial makeup of individual schools in Southern school districts. It required school boards to assign children and faculty to schools based on their race, now with the goal of meaningful racial mixing.

The initial effect of integration orders in Louisiana seemed promising. In February 1970, about a third of the state's Black children were attending majority-White public schools, although only about five percent of White students were attending majority Black public schools. A significant number of all-White schools and a much larger number of all-Black schools remained, but the contrast between what had prevailed before 1969 was striking. When the 1970–1971 school year began the following fall, the proportion of children in schools where the minority race composed at least one-tenth of the enrollment had risen to 63 percent.

2   It's typical of New Orleans and important to understand that there were the equivalent of public and private schools in the Catholic school system. There were the diocesan schools, which any Catholic could attend essentially free of charge, and private schools run by particular religious orders with selective admissions and tuition. For Black Catholic girls, the most elite high school was Xavier Prep, run by the Sisters of the Blessed Sacrament; for Black Catholic boys it was St. Augustine, run by the Josephite Fathers and Brothers. For White Catholic girls, it was Sacred Heart Academy; for White Catholic boys, it was Jesuit High School. The first three Black mayors of New Orleans were graduates of St. Augustine— Ernest "Dutch" Morial, Sidney Barthelemy, and Dutch's son Marc Morial.

3   *Davis v. East Baton Rouge School Board* (214 F. Supp. [E. D. La. 1963]) was filed in 1956. It was dismissed in 2003, although the federal district court retained jurisdiction and oversight of the school system until July 2007 in order to enforce the provisions of the 2003 agreement. The prolonged litigation ended a de jure system of all White and all Black schools. It ultimately resulted in a *de facto* system of predominately Black schools. In 2014, 80 percent of student enrollment in the parish was Black or other "people

of color." The Whites had gone elsewhere. For a summary and timeline of *Davis*, see http://www.coweninstitute.com/wp-content/uploads/2010/08/Louisiana-Desegregation-Case-Studies.pdf. For a more extensive treatment of the suit in the context of resistance to school integration in Louisiana, see Adam Fairclough, *Race & Democracy: The Civil Rights Struggle in Louisiana, 1915–1972* (University of Georgia Press, 2008).

[4] Although West came from Massachusetts, he was an unreconstructed Southerner. His appointment to the federal bench by John F. Kennedy was the consequence of his friendship with Russell Long, senior US senator from Louisiana, West's classmate at the LSU Law School and later his law partner. Repeatedly he ruled against plaintiffs asserting their civil rights and liberties. In early 1966, he even ruled against the US Department of Justice as it sought to implement as section of the 1965 Civil Rights Act (the Voting Rights Act). West called the act "flagrantly violative of the Constitution." His rulings were overturned so frequently that the *New York Times* published a story about it, which created a major hubbub in Baton Rouge.

[5] Scotlandville was in the northwest end of town; the historically Black Southern University was located there. Eden Park was just north and east of downtown. South Baton Rouge ran along the river from just south of downtown to the LSU campus and east a few blocks past I-10.

[6] Ducote subsequently founded and became the acting director of Advocates for Public Participation in Louisiana Education (APPLE), which lobbied to improve the state's public schools. Later, she became executive vice president and chief education lobbyist for the Louisiana Association of Business and Industry, and then first woman president of the Public Affairs Research Council of Louisiana, which did extensive research on education policy issues.

[7] In Ralph (Waldo Emerson) Ellison's *Invisible Man*, the unnamed protagonist attends an historically Black college loosely based, I think, on Tuskegee Institute, founded by Booker T. Washington. At one point, the president of the fictional school tells the protagonist, "This is a power set-up, son, and I'm at the controls." Speaking later of the way the world is, he adds, "I didn't make it, and I know I can't change it. But I've made my place in it and I'll have every Negro in the country hanging on tree limbs by morning if it means staying where I am." I used to wonder if *Invisible Man*, perhaps the greatest Black novel of the last century, was taught in English courses at Southern and Grambling, and if so, whether the teachers and students made the connection.

[8] The Southern University System had expanded in parallel with the LSU System. Both opened campuses in New Orleans in 1956, two years after the Supreme Court had declared separate but equal schools unconstitutional. Even less excusable was that both systems opened campuses in Shreveport in 1967. Enrollments in those SU campuses are about half as large as in the LSU campuses (LSU-NO was renamed UNO in 1974). The previously all-Black campuses are largely single-race. The previously all-White campuses enroll a significant percentage of Black students. The dual system is expensive to taxpayers and serves the interest of Black educators, not Black students. In 2011, when UNO was separated from the LSU System, State Senator Conrad Appel of Jefferson Parish, with the support of Governor Bobby Jindal, tried to combine UNO with SUNO as a way to save higher education dollars. His plan was withdrawn in both houses of the legislature for lack of support from his colleagues.

[9] And even those data are misleading about school integration, because about one in four Whites attend schools in the Zachary Community School District, which lies within the

parish but is separate from the East Baton Rouge Parish School System. School after school in the latter district is >90 percent Black. Baton Rouge High remains a bright spot: 44 percent White, 42 percent Black, 12 percent Asian, 2 percent Hispanic.

# CHAPTER 7

## Commitments[1]

The most famous commitment to a mental institution in Louisiana history occurred in 1959. I was working a summer job at the *Times-Picayune* in New Orleans and followed it closely. It was front page news from start to finish.

That year, Governor Earl K. Long was acting more erratically than usual. The most publicized of his antics was his infatuation with a Bourbon Street stripper named Blaze Starr, which became the basis for a 1989 film starring Paul Newman as "Uncle Earl." In early June, Long's wife, Blanche, with the complicity of Earl's nephew US Senator Russell Long, arranged to have him drugged, restrained, and flown to John Sealy Hospital in Galveston. By a combination of threats and the promise to commit himself voluntarily to Ochsner Hospital in New Orleans, Long secured his release.

He didn't honor his promise. After a day, he left Ochsner and headed for the state capital. Blanche had him intercepted at the East Baton Rouge Parish line by sheriff's deputies, who forced him into their squad car. They took him to city hall to be examined by the parish coroner plus a psychiatrist who had never met Long but rendered a verdict of paranoid schizophrenia on the spot. He was committed to Southeast Louisiana Hospital in Mandeville.

But Long was still governor. He called the board of state hospitals into meeting. They fired Jesse Bankston, then Director of Louisiana Hospitals, who had cooperated with Blanche in the initial kidnapping. Bankston's replacement then fired the director of Southeast and appointed a new director, who immediately determined that Long's condition didn't require hospitalization. Long was released and resumed his duties. After his term expired, he ran for Congress from the Eighth Congressional District and won the seat but died of a heart attack before he could serve.

Obscured by the sheer wackiness of that only-in-Louisiana story is an ugly reality that for almost a decade would command my attention. Legally, it was easy to commit persons against their will to mental institutions. And to a large extent, it was a power game. If someone—most often a family member—could persuade the parish coroner to agree, a psychiatrist could almost always be found to co-sign the coroner's warrant. My friend Bob Mellon, who was a lawyer in Livingston Parish just east of Baton Rouge, told me that the coroner there just kept a stack of presigned warrants in his office.[2]

There was no right to a judicial hearing before commitment. Once committed, by law the person could petition for a *habeas corpus* hearing, but in effect, few had the knowledge or power to exercise that right. So they faced indefinite detention. Their release depended on the arbitrary judgment of psychiatrists.

During those years with the ACLU, I dealt with many people in authority—mayors and city council members, sheriffs and police chiefs, school board members and principals, state legislators and, most often, district attorneys—but on the whole, psychiatrists struck me as the most dangerous of the lot.

*****

They struck Thomas Szasz that same way. A psychiatrist himself, who spent almost all his career on the faculty of the State University of New York at Syracuse, Szasz was and continues to be the *bete noir* of his profession. That's because he attacked it root and branch—namely, he denied that those behaviors that psychiatrists treated were properly called diseases or, more precisely, symptoms of diseases. Anxious to legitimate psychiatry by putting it on a medical basis, its practitioners were stung by his charges that they could point to no certain origins of the behaviors they regarded as treatable symptoms, that their diagnoses were arbitrary and unstable and their terminology was obscurantist.[3]

Civil libertarians didn't have a dog in that fight except when psychiatrists appropriated the coercive power of the state to impose their diagnoses and treatments on unwilling subjects. Unfortunately, they did so extensively and seemingly without qualms. When I began to address that gross injustice, the majority of commitments in Louisiana were involuntary. Further, if persons did commit themselves voluntarily, it was common for their keepers to change their status to involuntary by fiat…a judicial procedure was not required.

To acknowledge how much truth there was in Szasz's critique, all one need do is ask whether any other medical professionals—pediatricians, say, or cardiologists or orthopedists—would behave in such a fashion. Some physicians may be arrogant and dismiss as irrelevant what their patients think or want, but they don't get them locked up for indefinite periods of time, all in the name of their own good.

Szasz was born into a Jewish family in Budapest and emigrated to this country in 1938 at age eighteen. Perhaps that background explains his sensitivity to the stigmatizing of a minority population and the systematic denial of their legal rights. For in truth—and the federal judiciary would at last come to acknowledge this—a person accused of rape or murder had far more legal protection than a person accused of mental illness.

Szasz's public crusade began in 1958 with an article in the *Columbia Law Review*. Three years later, he testified at a US Senate hearing titled "The Constitutional Rights of the Mentally Ill." On that occasion, he argued that keeping people in mental hospitals involuntarily turned psychiatrists into wardens, not physicians.

These dates are instructive. Thanks to the Civil Rights Movement, there were stirrings of liberation among numerous oppressed populations—most notably women but also students, military personnel, and the physically disabled, among others. Each group came to have its own heroes and heroines—for the mentally ill, it was Szasz—but all the movements were indebted to the enormous courage and sacrifice of the South's Black nonviolent freedom fighters.

*****

I attended my first ACLU biennial convention in summer 1968. It was held on the University of Michigan campus in Ann Arbor. For a person fairly young in the work, the experience was electrifying. Every struggle of that apocalyptic year found its way into the meeting.

What a year it had already been! The Tet offensive starting January 31. The MLK assassination on April 4 and inner cities going up in flames. The student uprising at Columbia University in April and May. RFK's assassination on June 5. Less tragic clashes on a thousand fronts. No San Francisco "summer of love" that year. Flower Power had proved no match for the violence endemic to America since its origins and now nakedly manifest at home and abroad.

These many years later, I wonder how I remained engaged and still kept my balance. Most of the people I knew never engaged beyond conversation. Some who had, disengaged. Others lost their balance—there were far too many promising young people who crippled themselves with drugs or lost themselves in the labyrinths of Leftist polemics. My ballast, I think, was a habit of dutifulness. It kept me functioning reasonably well at home, at work, and in the public arena.

At the ACLU convention, everyone I met seemed grounded. When they talked about the issues—civil disobedience, the draft, repression of dissent, police brutality, the death penalty, many more—they were often passionate, but the passion was controlled by powerful intelligence and cogent reasoning. We weren't all lawyers; perhaps most of us weren't. But the tenor of the discourse, even when it wasn't about the law, was set by those with legal training and experience. Doubtless, there is a price to pay for such left-brained dominance, but losing one's way in utopian dreams or uncritical ideological allegiance is not one of them. If one needed a Guide to the Perplexed in those turbulent times, the ACLU policy manual was a good option.

It was the workshop on rights of the mentally ill that was most formative for me. While I had already become alert to some of the injustices they suffered, I had little knowledge of what remedies to seek and the resources available for the struggle. It was then that I first heard of Szasz's work and learned there were efforts nationwide to end abuse of involuntary commitments for indefinite lengths of time.

In Louisiana, that effort hadn't gotten started. The only person I discovered who was deeply interested was a Baton Rouge attorney named Sylvia Roberts, but Sylvia hadn't made much headway.[4] On a different front, there had been meaningful efforts to improve the conditions under which the mentally ill were kept. For this work, major credit goes to Victor Bussie, who led the state AFL-CIO for more than four decades, and his wife, Fran, who directed the organization's health endeavors. They were the main force behind the Louisiana Association for Mental Health (LAMH), using their political influence with governors and legislators to promote the well-being of the mentally ill.[5]

I wasn't able to get Louisiana out in front of the pace of developments in federal courts elsewhere, despite my attempts to find a willing plaintiff and an abortive attempt in the 1972 legislative session to build procedural safeguards into the commitment process. Finding a willing plaintiff brought me into contact with situations fraught with the complexities of difficult people and their frustrated family members. It was exhausting and unproductive of a case that could set legal precedent.

We might have had some success in the '72 session. I served on the Public Affairs Committee of LAMH from 1969 to 1972 and had persuaded the LAMH to tackle the civil liberties issues.[6] With LAMH on board, which meant Vic Bussie's support, the ACLU had a far better chance of passing a bill than if we were carrying the water by ourselves. Unfortunately, State Representative Woody Jenkins had offered himself to be point man for our cause then kept everything close to his vest and filed an unworkable proposal just before the filing deadline. Even I had to oppose it at the hearing, while still making it clear to a generally sympathetic committee that reform was urgently needed.

Two incidents from that occasion stick with me. One was talking with a Dr. Armistead, director of East Louisiana State Hospital at Jackson, outside the committee room. He was supportive of our effort. One reason was that, according to him, 20 percent of the residents in his facility weren't mentally ill, simply old. He explained that their relatives had gotten them committed to East rather than placing them in senior care facilities because as long as they were "patients," their social security payments were sent to them at their homes rather than to the care facility, which would have otherwise been the case. Having secured a power of attorney, the relatives were cashing the checks.

Armistead told me that these "patients" were receiving no treatment at East because they weren't ill, although they gradually deteriorated for lack of stimulation.

I thought to myself, as I listened to him, *Why, you chicken son of a bitch. You have the authority to stop this abuse* (such angry language went through my mind, and sometimes my lips, in those days). But apparently he believed that acquiescence was a condition of his employment, and I didn't want to alienate a useful ally.

The other incident was testimony from a representative of the state psychiatric association. He told the committee, "Let us practice psychiatry. You practice law." It seemed of no moment to him that he and his colleagues were using the coercive power of the law to impose their practice on non-consenting patients. The man's unreflective arrogance infuriated me.

Meanwhile, federal jurisprudence was moving in a direction that gave us increasing leverage. The earliest relevant cases had been decided by the US Court of Appeals in the District of Columbia.[7] Contesting practices at St. Elizabeth's Hospital there, they resulted in two requirements that later court decisions made universally applicable in the United States, not only for the mentally ill but also for the mentally retarded. One was individualized and appropriate treatment programs. The other was placement in the least restrictive appropriate environment.

The next milestone was *Wyatt v. Stickney* (325 F. Supp. 781, 1971), a ruling by Frank Minis Johnson Jr., the extraordinary federal judge for the Middle District of Alabama, of whom Bill Moyers said he "altered forever the face of the South" and to whom Bill Clinton awarded the Presidential Medal of

Freedom in 1995. In his decision, Judge Johnson declared that if a state institution couldn't provide care according to standards that became known as the Wyatt rules, it couldn't hold people against their will.

It was not until 1975, however, with the US Supreme Court's ruling in *O'Connor v. Donaldson* (422 US 563), that the Holy Grail was attained. *Donaldson* established nationwide the rule that persons can be committed involuntarily only if they are a demonstrable danger to themselves or others. And "demonstrable" means convincing to a judge in an evidentiary procedure during which persons are entitled to counsel.

In 1977, the legislature brought Louisiana into conformity with the new federal jurisprudence. The standard became demonstrably dangerous to self or others, or gravely disabled, with good due process guarantees for the hearing. Someone could be held for at most seven days on an emergency intervention but not for longer without a judicial finding of demonstrable danger. If there was an involuntarily commitment, the law mandated a court review after the first 60 days, then the next 120, and then 180 forever after. The practice of converting voluntary to involuntary commitments by fiat also ended.

The impact of these new due process and treatment requirements was to empty out the large institutions, many of which were in small towns at some distance from the patients' homes. The patient population of East fell from five thousand to five hundred within three years.

But just because people were not demonstrably dangerous to themselves or others didn't mean they needed no help. Notwithstanding many exceptions, people had been institutionalized for a reason. Families were understandably unable or unwilling to care for difficult and uncooperative relatives. Care should have been provided by support systems featuring small group homes and regular medical supervision, but states and cities failed to establish such systems adequate to the need. Consequently, all too often, the phrase "return to the community" was a euphemism. The new address for multitudes of those released from the institutions was the streets.

I don't think that outcome bothered Szasz. His extreme libertarianism affirmed people's right to be as self-destructive as they wish without interference. In 1976, when he gave a talk at LSU in connection with the publication by our press of his *Karl Kraus and the Soul-Doctors: A Pioneer Critic and His Criticism of Psychiatry and Psychoanalysis*, I asserted during the Q & A that the state might intervene in a very limited way to prevent a person's suicide. In many instances, I pointed out, suicide is an impulsive, not a considered act, and a brief cooling off period often results in a change of mind. He would have none of that argument.

Whatever Szasz did or didn't feel, I was bothered by the unintended consequence of the part I had played, however small, in the movement to secure civil liberties for those accused of being mentally ill. I invested a lot of myself in promoting civil liberties in a troubled place at a troubled time, but I was not ideologically motivated. I did so because I believed that each of us is responsible for the well-being of every other member of the human family, and protecting people from the illegitimate exercise of state power struck me as a worthwhile way to be my brother's keeper. I regret that in this case protecting people from one threat to their well-being exposed many of them to other threats.

Still, I would not undo what we did. People shouldn't be stripped of their autonomy the way psychiatrists, appropriating state power, stripped their patients of self-rule. Being our brother's jailor makes a mockery of being our brother's keeper.

*****

Just how avid some psychiatrists were to be their brothers' jailors was made clear to me by a bill filed in the 1972 legislative session.

To understand this story, one needs to know how often Louisiana legislators took no responsibility for the bills they filed. It didn't take much political clout to get a state senator or representative to submit a bill prepared by others without even reading it. That was a practice I found reprehensible, a flagrant dereliction of duty. I remember once trying to speak with Billy Tauzin, then a state representative from Lafourche Parish (later a US congressman), about a bill he had filed. He told me, "That's the DAs' bill."

I replied, "It's got your name on it."

In a sharp tone, he repeated, "That's the DAs' bill," and turned away.

One day, in the midst of the '72 session, I got a call from Kendall Vick on behalf of Michael O'Keefe, a state senator from New Orleans. Kendall had been general counsel of the state ACLU before joining the attorney general's office when Billy Guste assumed the office that very year. Kendall's wife, Kathy (whose father was my dentist when

I was a child), worked for O'Keefe. So it was that when O'Keefe finally looked at a bill he had filed at the request of Louis Hyde, Criminal Sheriff of Orleans Parish, and got worried about what he was seeing, I was the one asked to evaluate its implications.

Reading it worried me as well. The bill called for the establishment of a special institution within the Department of Corrections under the direct control of a Commission on Social Delinquency. The five-member commission was to be composed of two psychiatrists, a PhD psychologist, a corrections professional, and an attorney. To this new institution, a person in the criminal justice pipeline could be diverted, given a sentence of indeterminate length, subjected to a behavior modification program, and released only when the mental health professionals decided that he was ready to return to society. Criteria for diversion were extremely broad: anyone who had committed two felonies of any kind (writing two bad checks for more than $100, for example) was eligible.

The hearing on O'Keefe's bill was scheduled for the following afternoon. I did what I always did under such circumstances: I sought help from friends on the law school faculty, in this instance, Lee Hargrave. Lee found a relevant case, an inmate suit against something called the Patuxent Institute in Maryland. As described in the case report, that facility fit the description of what was contemplated in O'Keefe's bill. The suit alleged that the treatment programs at Patuxent were, in reality, a combination of abuse and neglect, and there had been no demonstrable payoffs either for society or those diverted to the facility.

Given my twenty-four-hour deadline, that case plus my own analysis of the bill from a civil liberties viewpoint were all I could bring to the hearing. Fortunately, they were enough. Sheriff Hyde was ill prepared to present the bill, which he identified at the hearing as the work of psychiatrists at the Tulane Medical School. In my turn, I spoke of the good intentions of the bill (which I didn't believe for an instant) but indicated its potential hazards and the questionable results at Patuxent.

The committee on which O'Keefe sat was receptive to my remarks. At O'Keefe's request, it gave the bill a favorable report only with the proviso that it wouldn't be moved forward until it was amended to address the concerns I had raised. O'Keefe assigned that task to me. Again, with guidance from law school friends, I worked it over. I tightened the criteria for divergence, required release no later than the maximum sentence for the crime committed, and most importantly, made participation and continuation in the program voluntary.

The bill as amended in these ways never went to the floor. Apparently, the Tulane psychiatrists had no interest in that kind of program.[8]

Less than two years later, such programs were under heavy attack across the country. Indeed, they had largely been discredited, at least in the form proposed. In March 1974, the Federal Bureau of Prisons ended its most heralded program, the Special Treatment and Rehabilitative Program at the prison in Springfield, Missouri. That same year, the Law Enforcement Assistance Administration, pipeline of federal funds to criminal justice systems, announced the termination of funding for almost all behavior modification programs in

US prisons. As for the ability of mental health professionals to decide when a person is fit to reenter society, again in the same year the American Psychiatric Association's Task Force on the Clinical Aspects of Violent Individuals reported, "Neither psychiatrists nor anyone else have reliably demonstrated an ability to predict future violence or 'dangerousness.' Neither has any special psychiatric 'expertise' in this area been established."[9]

Behind these acknowledgements of failure was a reality so grotesque that even "success" wouldn't have justified it in any traditional value system.

Aversion therapy entailed the most blatant abuses. At the Iowa Security Medical Facility, for example, apomorphine was injected into non-consenting prisoners as "treatment" for such antisocial acts as giving cigarettes against orders, talking, and swearing. The effect was fifteen minutes of uninterrupted vomiting. At two California prison medical facilities, at Vacaville and Atascadero, the drug succinylcholine chloride was used. Injected into bound prisoners, its effect was a rapid paralysis beginning at the extremities. Then for two minutes the diaphragm would stop pumping and breathing cease. During suffocation, the doctor would command the prisoners to become obedient to authority. Besides drugs, in some instances, electric shock and even psychosurgery was used.

That was the garish side of behavior modification. More common was behavior modification through operant conditioning, fathered by B. F. Skinner. In the prison setting, however, whatever virtues claimed for it—e.g., that it replaces a punishment model with positive reinforcement—were undermined by the uncontestable fact that the subjects were under the coercive control of their handlers. And the primary control their handlers had was complete discretion about when the prisoners would be released.

I could continue to throw light on this darkest corner of what Szasz called "the therapeutic state." For my purpose, however, which has been to explain why opposition to the hubris of the psychiatric profession was important to me, the foregoing should suffice. I'll conclude this section with the words of Roosevelt Murray, who at age seventeen was convicted of unauthorized use of a vehicle (i.e. joy-riding), received a four-year sentence, and was then diverted to Patuxent. In 1976, he testified before the Senate Judicial Proceedings Committee of the Maryland Legislature:

> As one who has spent 10 long, miserable years in Patuxent's tenacious grip, I can attest to its mindless and incredible waste of human lives… It is a story of human tragedy on a truly massive scale, the liberals' dream turned into some Orwellian nightmare, of unbelievable suffering of fellow human beings like myself, trapped by fate and relegated to a future without hope should they dare resist efforts to alter their minds and personalities.

*****

I was on sabbatical leave in Santa Cruz, California for the academic year 1972–1973. Shortly after I resumed my duties in the 1973 fall semester, I learned that an LSU student being held on a coroner's warrant had committed suicide in the downtown jail, which occupied several floors above the courtrooms.

The details were gruesome. A sitting judge kept hearing a pounding noise, so he sent the deputy assigned to his courtroom to investigate. The source of the noise had been the student's pounding his head against the bars of his cell. No one had come to investigate before the judge dispatched his deputy. By that time, it was too late; the man was dead.

As soon as I heard what had happened, I telephoned the coroner, Dr. Hypolite Landry, because by then, state law forbade housing in a penal facility anyone being held under civil commitment. I'm not sure that Landry even knew the law, but he didn't argue. Instead, he said that there were no hospital beds open to him, so he had had no other option. I pointed out that leaving the man alone would have been a better option. What worse could he have done to himself? "He might have run into the street and gotten killed," was Landry's reply.

"We all could do that," I responded.

Knowing that he was liable, Landry promised me that in the future he wouldn't house in the jail anyone picked up on a coroner's warrant. He called me back shortly thereafter and told me he had persuaded the director of Earl K. Long Hospital to set aside six beds in a closed ward for his use.[10]

Just which psychiatrist co-signed the coroner's warrant in this case I didn't ascertain. I suspect, however, that it was Dr. John Kuehn, a psychiatrist who directed mental health services at LSU from 1966 to 1975. I hadn't met Kuehn before this incident, although I was well-acquainted with his assistant, Suzanne Jensen, a clinical psychologist. She and I were members of the congregation at the Catholic Student Center.

I met Kuehn because he invited me to attend a meeting related to the student's death. Besides Kuehn, present were Jensen and Peter Soderberg, dean of the College of Education—the dead man had been a student in that college. The focus of the meeting, I discovered, was not what had happened after the unfortunate young man had been picked up on the coroner's warrant. Rather, it was to anticipate psychotic episodes on campus that would require intervention. Kuehn's idea was to institute a system of comprehensive record-keeping on students who showed signs of mental instability.

Jensen and Soderberg supported the idea. I said it raised concerns about students' privacy, since we weren't talking about medical records of students who sought mental health services, but files on potentially any student at LSU. I suspect that it was precisely to learn of, and perhaps overcome, such resistance to Kuehn's proposal that I had been invited to the meeting.

The meeting ended with my volunteering to draft a proposal that would adequately address my reservations. I never did draft it, partly because I couldn't make the time, partly because my heart wasn't in it. To my knowledge, the proposed scheme was dropped.

\*\*\*\*\*

As this chapter has indicated, the ambition to create a society devoid of aberration and to quarantine mentally distressed people for their own good struck me as a dangerous ambition. But I would be remiss in not looking at the pressures under which people like Kuehn worked. As he pointed out years later, he had been hired by LSU not long after Charles Whitman climbed into the tower at the University of Texas and shot forty-six people, sixteen of whom died. "At the time of my hiring, LSU had the expectation that one of my key functions would be to triage for dangerousness… We have a tower at LSU too!"[11]

Kuehn recalled that "I had excellent support from campus security and the East Baton Rouge Parish coroner and sheriff, so we could easily remove dangerous students from campus or get them hospitalized either privately or at state facilities." And he deplored the changes that had occurred by 2000, the year of his published recollection: "Unfortunately, in recent years another of the results of deinstitutionalization and marginalization of psychiatry by managed care is the severe difficulty we now have in arranging [involuntary] inpatient care for college students, most of whom have no or inadequate insurance."

How many students Kuehn had removed and how dangerous they were is hard to know. In 1969, Kuehn co-authored an article in the *American Journal of Psychiatry* entitled "Management of the College Student with Homicidal Impulses—The 'Whitman Syndrome.'"[12] In it he presented three case studies of "globally hostile students," meaning students angry at the world, all three of whom possessed firearms. The cases seem convincing.

It's worth noting, however, that a man calling himself Case no. 2 started a blog on July 31, 2008, in which he asserted that he was the person so described in Kuehn's 1969 study, and he disputed Kuehn's presentation of the facts, including his access to firearms. Whether he was Case no. 2 (Kuehn denied it), it seems true that he was Kuehn's patient during his freshman year and that he had to leave LSU as a consequence of Kuehn's handling of his case. After four decades, he remained bitter: "'Tell me Dr. Kuehn, how would you feel if a physician treated you as you treated me, during your freshman year of college?'... The past never changes and thus Dr. Kuehn's legacy will forever be marred and marked with the indelible stain which he alone placed upon his soul. The fact that Dr. Kuehn is in such deep denial and apparently suffers no remorse is troubling. I would be ashamed and would find it impossible to live with the burden of such guilt on my conscience."[13]

The impossibility of arriving at an unequivocal judgment in this matter accords with my own experience with troubled people and those authorized to "treat" them. I derived from it three lessons that still strike me as useful. One is humility. Human reality is too complex and murky to justify confidence in our judgments. The second, a corollary of the first, is that one must carefully limit the power of those who wish to impose their judgments on others. Finally, if the social conditions we have created keep producing large numbers of distressed, often violent individuals, expecting (and empowering) a profession to get people to properly "adjust" to those conditions is at best a Band-

Aid and, at worst, a major obstacle to our collective quest for sanity.

---

[1] This chapter focuses exclusively on civil commitments. For a discussion of criminal commitments and how Louisiana finally rectified the gross injustices associated with them, see Chapter 3 and especially footnote 3.

[2] From 1970 through 1975, 11,082 persons were committed to Southeast Louisiana Hospital; 4,651 were committed on coroners' warrants.

[3] On those last two points, Warren Burger, later to become Chief Justice of the US Supreme Court, agreed. In a 1961 case he heard when a Circuit Court judge, he complained, "No rule of law can possibly be sound or workable which is dependent upon the terms of another discipline whose members are in profound disagreement about what those terms mean... [The term 'mental disease'], which has no fixed, agreed or accepted definition in the discipline which is called upon to supply expert testimony [in court cases] and which, as we have seen, is literally 'subject to change without notice,' is a tenuous and indeed dangerously vague term to be a critical part of a rule of law on criminal responsibility" (Jeffrey Oliver, "The Myth of Thomas Szasz," *The New Atlantis*, number 13, Summer 2006).

[4] Sylvia graduated from the Tulane Law School, where she made law review, and then studied at the Montpellier School of Law in France, which was founded in the twelfth century and has been distinguished ever since. She told me that, despite her qualifications, when she sought her first job, all she was offered was the position of law librarian. Now, when I hear loose talk of how there has been no meaningful change in this country, I like to recount stories like Sylvia's.

5   I take this opportunity to honor Vic and Fran. They were necessarily political to their core, which meant that at times they made alliances with highly corrupt politicians, Edwin Edwards being the outstanding example. But in addition to promoting the good of working people, they advocated for better schools, the protection of the mentally ill and the mentally retarded, and other worthy causes. Cautiously but significantly, they placed themselves and the state AFL-CIO on the right side of racial integration. I wasn't always on easy terms with the Bussies, but I am proud to have known them.

6   In the summer 1970 edition of Target, the LAMH newsletter, Homer Bartee, LAMH president, wrote that there was a need for a comprehensive mental health bill and the organization should begin working on it now.

7   *Rouse v. Cameron* 373 F.2d 451 (1966) and *Lake v. Cameron* 331 F.2d 771 (1966).

8   I later learned that Tulane psychiatrists, led by Dr. Robert G. Heath, had performed craniotomies on one hundred patients over the course of three decades beginning in 1950 for the purpose of subcortical electrical stimulation. Many of their subjects were poor patients at New Orleans Charity Hospital. Despite early claims, the therapeutic benefits of these experiments were minimal. Further, two subjects died of brain abscesses after the electrode implantations and others had seizures. More important, there was no effort to meet what today would be considered the most basic requirements for federal authorization of human experimentation. For a detailed history and description of what I predict most readers will find appalling conduct, see Alan A. Baumeister, "The Tulane Electrical Brain Stimulation Program: A Historical Case Study in Medical Ethics," *Journal of the History of the Neurosciences* 2000, vol. 9, no. 3, pp. 262–78 (available online at http://www.lsu.edu/psychology/

documents/baumeister/Tulane%20Electrical%20Brain%20 Stimulation%20Program.pdf). Tulane, however, never lost faith in Heath's work despite growing evidence of its failures and ethical abuses. Five years after he retired in 1980, the university awarded him an honorary doctorate and created the Robert G. Heath Chair in Psychiatry and Neurology.

[9] For this and the following information on behavior modification programs in the prisons, I am indebted to two sources. The greater debt is to Arpiar G. Sanders, "Behavior Therapy in Prisons: Walden II or Clockwork Orange?", a paper presented at the Eighth Annual Convention of the Association for the Advancement of Behavior Therapy in 1974 and updated through 1975. It may still be available through the ACLU's National Prison Project. Also Philip J. Hilts, *Behavior Mod* (New York, Harper's Magazine Press, 1974), Chapter 6.

[10] During the 1974 session of the Louisiana Legislature, the sheriffs got a bill filed that would give them immunity from any lawsuits arising from incidents in the parish jails, which are under their legal authority and control. At the hearing on the bill, I told the story I have just recounted as an example of the gross negligence for which the sheriffs were asking to be held free of accountability. The bill did not get a favorable report and thus died in committee.

[11] *Psychiatric News*, September 15, 2000, letter to the editor.

[12] *American Journal of Psychiatry* 1969; 125:1594–159.

[13] http://thewhitmansyndrome.blogspot.com/.

# CHAPTER 8

# Struggling on Multiple Fronts

The Voting Rights Act of 1965 was the political gamechanger. The Civil Rights Act Congress passed the year before had provided the tool racial and ethnic minorities (and, in the case of employment, women) needed to overcome multiple social and economic forms of discrimination, but the Voting Rights Act cleared a path to power. That's why there were efforts to subvert it when it was passed and why those efforts have been revived since the US Supreme Court, to its disgrace, gutted the act in 2013.[1]

What made the act so effective was Section 5. It required certain states and counties, originally almost all in the Deep South, to preclear with the US Department of Justice any changes to voting laws and practices that might disenfranchise racial minority voters. Black registration in the covered states soared. In 1964, fewer than 7 percent of eligible blacks were registered to vote in Mississippi; by the end of 1966, the figure had risen to nearly 60 percent. During the same period in Alabama, registration rates climbed from just below 20 percent to just above 50 percent. According to the statistical estimates of the Voter Education Project, by 1972, more than a million and a half Blacks had become registered voters in the South. In Louisiana 57 percent of voting-age Blacks had registered (compared to 78 percent of eligible White voters).

Black enfranchisement quickly began to change electoral politics in the South. Jim Clark, sheriff of Dallas County, Alabama, who in March 1965 had led the attacks on voting rights marchers in Selma, was out of office the next year, thanks to eight thousand new Black voters. George Wallace, who swore after he lost his first bid for governor of Alabama in 1958 that he would never be "out-niggered again," managed to stay on top of Alabama politics in the 1970s by abandoning such rhetoric and eventually apologizing to Black leaders: "I was wrong. Those days are over, and they ought to be over."

The new Black political power had two goals. One was to change the tone of political life and the behavior of White officials. The other was to elect Blacks to public office. It didn't take long to see changes of tone and behavior because it became an increasingly risky electoral strategy to intentionally alienate a sizable percentage of the electorate. Electing Blacks to public office was more difficult. The strategy of White resistance was to create multi-member election districts large enough to keep Blacks in the minority and make candidates run at large.

In the mid-1960s, state legislatures were under pressure by the federal courts to end the over-representation of rural residents and underrepresentation of urban residents that resulted from their refusal to redistrict as populations moved to the cities. In 1966, the federal courts ruled unconstitutional the redistricting the Louisiana legislature had done after the 1960 census and mandated a second redistricting to give each resident equal representation. The legislature kept the same number of seats in both chambers but created some multi-member districts in the urban areas such as Metro New Orleans, Shreveport, and Baton Rouge. Only one Black reached the legislature under that scheme. In 1967, Ernest "Dutch" Morial was elected to represent a House district in New Orleans, the first Black to serve in the state legislature since Reconstruction. (He was later elected a state district judge and then, in 1977, won his race for mayor, another first.)

When legislatures were next required to redistrict using the 1970 census data, the Constitutional concern was no longer urban-rural inequality but racial inequality. In *Whitcomb v. Chavis* (1971), the US Supreme Court didn't prohibit multi-member districts, but it did make them "justiciable," meaning occasion for judicial review to determine if they violated the Voting Rights Act.

Louisiana elects its state officials every four years in odd-numbered years. With the November 1971 election looming, the legislature adopted a plan that almost everyone knew wouldn't survive Justice Department scrutiny. Federal Judge E. Gordon West then intervened, declaring that even if the US Attorney General hadn't found the plan racially discriminatory, he would have voided it because it so egregiously violated the principle of one man-one vote.

West appointed Ed Steimel, executive director of the nonprofit Public Affairs Research Council, as the court's Special Master to draw up a plan. Steimel submitted one based on single-member districts. Over strenuous protests by, among others, Louisiana AFL-CIO President Victor Bussie, and perhaps motivated by *Whitcomb*, West approved the plan. Black leaders applauded his decision, with good reason. When the 1972 legislature convened, there were one Black senator—Sidney Bartholomew from New Orleans—and seven Black representatives—Johnnie Jackson Jr., Theodore "Teddy" Marchand, Louis Charbonnet III and Dorothy Mae Taylor from New Orleans, Johnnie Jones and Richard Turnley Jr. from Baton Rouge, and Alphonse Jackson Jr. from Shreveport.

On the job, at least, the Black legislators were accepted as colleagues. In 1990, a retrospective Johnnie Jones answered a schoolgirl who asked him if there had been racism among the legislators when he served, "If there was, I tell you, it wasn't among the legislators. I couldn't find it."[2] Naïve as Jones's response sounds, it probably reflected his experience with some accuracy. Given the lawmaking process, the support of their Black colleagues was worth trying to win for bills that White legislators wanted to pass. And during the time I spent at the Capitol lobbying for the ACLU, I never saw any legislator publicly treat another one disrespectfully, no matter what they might say in private. That was the culture.

Blacks had greater difficulty gaining representation on municipal governing bodies and school boards. In Baton Rouge, for example, candidates had to run at large for the city-parish council and the school board and also for city and state district judgeships.[3]

Legal challenges to at-large districts hinged on the contention that Blacks' newly affirmed freedom to vote was insufficient if their votes could never elect candidates willing to take their interests into consideration. The behavior of the East Baton Rouge Parish School Board toward racial integration, which I discussed in Chapter 6, was proof that this contention had merit. Federal courts, however, were slow to rule that the fact situations presented to them merited relief under the Voting Rights Act. The conditions that would warrant relief from minority vote dilution became the subject of intense and increasingly complicated litigation, both with respect to at-large or multimember-district elections and with respect to allegedly gerrymandered single-member districts.[4]

What the courts did declare early on was that at-large schemes *might* violate the Voting Rights Act, which authorizes federal action "to make a vote effective." Thus, in *Allen v. State Board of Elections* (1969), the US Supreme Court declared that the State of Mississippi couldn't implement a change to its election code requiring all county supervisors to run county-wide without first submitting that change to the US Justice Department for its approval, as required by Section 5 of the Voting Rights Act. But *Allen* didn't declare that at-large schemes were *prima facie* violations. And as mentioned previously, in *Whitcomb v. Chavis* (1971), the court said that "the validity of multi-member districts is justiciable, but a challenger has the burden of proving that such districts unconstitutionally operate to dilute or cancel the voting strength of racial or political groups." It was only in 1973, in a case out of San Antonio, that the court finally concluded that the burden of proof had been met: Mexican-Americans "are effectively removed from the political processes of Bexar [County] in violation of all the *Whitcomb* standards." It concluded that single-member districts were required to remedy "the effects of past and present discrimination."[5]

As late as 1980, the US Supreme Court was still requiring proof that a challenged election structure was designed or maintained intentionally to dilute minority voting strength. Even so, the number of Black elected officials in the states designated in Section 5 of the Voting Rights Act had climbed from seventy-two in 1965, before the act was passed, to almost one thousand ten years later. Then in its Voting Rights Act of 1982, Congress made it easier to challenge schemes like at-large districts by changing the standard of proof from a showing of intention to a showing of result. That legislation, along with a 1986 Supreme Court decision that streamlined the required demonstration, sparked widespread changes from at-large to single-member district elections.

The Baton Rouge City Council elected its members at large for multiple seats in each of the three city wards. In 1968, Joe Delpit ran for Baton Rouge City Council in Ward 1, the most populous. "I didn't think I could win because no Black person ever had," he said later. Delpit had inherited from his father a thriving chicken restaurant in South Baton Rouge, and he had built a solid political base in that Black residential area.[6] Other influential Blacks in the city, including T. J. Jemison,[7] encouraged him to run. So his Black support was unified, but he needed White support as well. He found it among Whites associated with the Baton Rouge Human Relations Council, which was very active in the closing years of the decade. The argument that it is only fair that Blacks have at least some representation in their city government struck a chord. Even one of my next-door neighbors, who grew up in Philadelphia, Mississippi and had difficulty adjusting to the enormous changes occurring around him, said he would vote for Delpit for just that reason.

And so Delpit won the seat, which he occupied until his election in November 1975 to the state House of Representatives, replacing Johnnie Jones and serving there for 16 years. Delpit was a gifted politician and rose to leading positions on both on the council and in the state house. At the start, there was some harassment, but not from his fellow council members. He wasn't able to prevent them from adopting an ordinance that made parents criminally responsible for crimes of their minor children—indeed, he seemed not to understand its racist import until I pointed it out in my testimony opposing it. But he played a major role in changing the rules governing police use of lethal force after city police killed two unarmed Black youth in 1969 and one in 1973.[8]

In 1971, Federal District Judge E. Gordon West ordered the city council to come up with a reapportionment plan before the 1972 election. Early in 1972, led by Mayor Woody Dumas, the city council voted to create single-member districts in each ward instead of retaining ward-wide elections to multiple seats. There were objections both on the council and from outside parties, most notably the Public Affairs Research Council. Nonetheless, the new system, which was approved by the Justice Department, was implemented in time for the August primaries.

The results of the primaries, run-offs, and then the general election in November were that newcomers won eight of the twelve council seats. Of those, three were African Americans—William Winfield, Benjamin Harbor, and Jewel Newman. Delpit was one of the four incumbents who won re-election. So Blacks finally were represented roughly in proportion to their percentage of the population.

The East Baton Rouge Parish School Board stubbornly clung to its system of electing multiple members at large from each ward. It was the state legislature that finally forced it to adopt single-member districts. In 1981, it passed a law requiring the board to develop a plan by the end of the year to divide the parish into single-member districts "drawn with as equal population as possible, utilizing population figures from the 1980 United States government census." It also stipulated that the plan had to be submitted for approval to the East Baton Rouge Parish legislative delegation and gave the delegation authority to develop an alternative plan if it didn't approve what was submitted. In the general election of 1982, voters elected their school board from single-member districts.

The same struggle to win Black representation on city and parish governing bodies and school boards was waged in regard to the election of judges. At-large elections for judicial posts were the norm across Louisiana, with the desired result—exclusion of Blacks. When I lived there, the Baton Rouge City Court had three judges and the 19th Judicial District Court of East Baton Rouge Parish had thirteen judges, all of them White. A series of legal and legislative remedies, all attempted after I was no longer doing civil liberties work, achieved little. Baton Rouge elected its first Black City Court judge, Freddie Pitcher, Jr., in 1987, shortly I left the state. By 1988, of 156 district court judgeships outside of Orleans Parish, only two Blacks had ever been elected. Of the forty-eight Court of Appeal judgeships in the state, only one judge was Black, and there had never been a Black on the

State Supreme Court (there is one now). The Louisiana bench still is White far beyond the percentage of the population that race constitutes.

*****

The right of males to grow their hair any length they chose wasn't my most pressing concern, but during the five years that calls to the Baton Rouge Chapter of the ACLU came to my home phone, the single most frequent complaint was that some authority was requiring the aggrieved caller to cut his hair. Ragni, Rado and MacDermot, the creators of *Hair*, nailed it: hair was at the center of the sixties' youth culture.[9]

What I liked about the issue was that it cut across lines of race and class and, without inflicting significant harm, introduced White middle-class kids to the reality of unreasonable authority. Together with the risk of being drafted into a war that was increasingly losing its moral suasion, that experience alienated them from the culture of their parents and sensitized them to its graver injustices, of which they hitherto had been oblivious.

I could do nothing for those in private employment who complained that their supervisors ordered them to cut their hair. It was different if a public agency was involved. One man had been denied unemployment benefits because the person he dealt with at the agency maintained that he couldn't seriously be looking for work if he had long hair. I was able to get him relief without legal recourse, as I recall. Another, enrolled at the state-supported trade school in Baton Rouge, was ordered to cut his hair, purportedly because long hair posed a hazard—it might get caught in a machine in the shop. We resolved that problem by having the man agree to coil his hair under a cap.

We had less success with the Baton Rouge Police Department. In January 1969, the department decreed that sideburns had to be short and that mustaches were only acceptable for policemen who had them before the decree. We sent letters to Major R. Stanley Trigg, who issued the order, and Mayor Dumas. In the related news release, I said that "no public servant should be deprived of his rights unless it is necessary for the performance of his duties. The ACLU finds it hard to understand how sideburns or a mustache can interfere with police functioning."

The Baton Rouge City Patrolmen's Association failed to support officers unhappy with the rule. Its president said in a letter to the editor, "It appears fashionable today for some to dissent merely for the sake of dissension; to create disunity and chaos in the name of freedom and liberty; and to encourage extremism in the name of individualism." No officers called for our assistance. As time went by and facial hair became more common, however, mustaches became acceptable.

The most frequent complaints we received about hair were from students in public schools. At first, the parish school district had no uniform policy. Decisions about students' appearance—both clothing and grooming—were at the discretion of the school principals, and they exercised their authority arbitrarily and often capriciously. Many people think that the first step toward correcting an injustice is to change the law, but actually the first step is to get a law—any law—to constrain individual discretion. The second step is to make sure the people administering it know what the law is. The third is to get them to abide by it. Only after all those steps have been taken can one focus on the justice of the law itself. In this instance, we had to start with step one.

Litigation wasn't a viable option. The Chicago ACLU had secured a favorable ruling from the Seventh Circuit Court of Appeals, but other circuits, including the Fifth (ours) didn't agree, and the US Supreme Court passed on the opportunity to harmonize the varying lower court decisions when it wouldn't hear an appeal to reinstate a vacated injunction against school hair regulations in El Paso.[10] Persuasion was our only recourse.

Three women—Fannie Godwin, Audrey Kirby and Helen Wagster—whose children had encountered difficulties in Baton Rouge schools, led our efforts for more than six years. They were feisty, funny, and clever. They began to attend regularly the school board meetings and delighted in upsetting its members.

One of their initiatives was to create a student rights pamphlet complete with delightful drawings, such as a grossed-out school official searching a student's locker from which wafted the noxious smells of unwashed gym socks. In late 1969, they distributed it at Baker High School, whose principal they regarded as especially authoritarian. It created quite a stir. What caused the most outcry was its first page, which explained that students didn't have to salute the flag or recite the Pledge of Allegiance. That right had been established back in 1943 in *West Virginia State Board of Education v. Barnette* in response to the religious objections of Jehovah's Witnesses. That legal history was unknown locally, however, and to those already upset by the rapid cultural changes they were living through, the handbook seemed like still another attack on the America they knew.

In 1972, the parish school board adopted by a 7–3 vote a uniform code on student hair and dress. Males could have mustaches and hair over their ears and down to their shoulders, but no further. Beards were forbidden. While restrictive, the new rules ended the varying and capricious dicta of individual principals. A proper resolution of the issue, as well as others regarding student rights, took three more years. Continuous agitation and challenges finally persuaded the school board to create a student bill of rights and responsibilities. Howard Marcellus, Jr., then a middle school principal, was chosen to lead the project. That was a fortunate choice for us, since he was open to our concerns about free speech and due process as well as personal expression. We didn't get everything we wanted. For instance, the document didn't require a search warrant to look into a student's locker, but it did require that a written memo of cause be kept on file.

And regarding the matter of hair, the stated policy was that you [students] "can determine your dress and grooming as long as your appearance does not endanger the health or safety of others, or disrupt the orderly process of learning." The final draft was submitted to the school board in December 1974 and was approved to take effect in the 1975–1976 school year.

Beyond the school yard, out on the city sidewalks, long hair could occasionally lead to arrest. People couldn't be charged with looking like hippies, but vagrancy laws were so broadly written that they provided sufficient cover for prejudicial police behavior.

Such was the case when, on February 10, 1969, Baton Rouge police arrested three young adults from Denver who had come to build a geodesic dome for a man in nearby Port Vincent. John and Carol Wagner and Rodney Bowers were downtown after having tried to cash a $50 payroll check. I arranged for my friend Marcia Mellon, whose own hippie proclivities had led her to stop practicing law on a regular basis, to represent them. She filed a writ of *habeas corpus* in district court on the twelfth, arguing that the three were being held without probable cause. The next day, they were released on their own recognizance. In a statement to the news media, I asked, "Why then were they arrested? The answer is clear: they had long hair and looked like hippies, obviously a crime in the eyes of local law enforcement."

I told the media that the ACLU had entered the case as the first step in a campaign to halt indiscriminate and illegal use of the vagrancy law. But the assistant city prosecutor announced that he would drop the charges, ostensibly because they had $50 and a place to stay. So that case didn't become the vehicle for our ultimately successful challenge of Louisiana's vagrancy statute and the abuses it made possible.

*****

In Europe, vagrancy statutes were enacted after the enormous death toll of the 1348–49 bubonic plague created a labor shortage. They were intended to prevent serfs previously bound to a single master's land from seeking work on better terms elsewhere. So, too, vagrancy statutes were updated by states of the former Confederacy immediately after the Civil War to regain control of emancipated Black labor. Even the Freedmen's Bureau, which had a mandate to protect Blacks from a hostile Southern environment, cooperated with Southern authorities in rounding up black "vagrants" and placing them in contract work to revive production on the plantations.

Eight of the nine states that used vagrancy laws in this way also instituted convict leasing—the hiring out of convict labor for work on plantations or public works projects. This created a financial incentive for the states to arrest and convict Black men. In 1898, some 73 percent of Alabama's annual state revenue came from convict leasing. So using their vagrancy statutes, states like Louisiana were able to reintroduce slavery on a smaller scale.

In 1928, Alabama was the last state officially to end hired convict labor; in practice, it didn't end until the start of World War II. A legacy of those benighted times was that the vagrancy statutes, which remained on the books, usually were written with a breadth and vagueness intended to give police a pretext to haul into the station anyone they viewed as suspicious. In 1972, the US Supreme Court invalidated a Jacksonville, Florida, statute—and by extension, all such statutes—"for vagueness, in that it 'fails to give a person of ordinary intelligence fair notice that his contemplated conduct is forbidden by the statute' [the quote is from the ruling in an earlier case], it encourages arbitrary and erratic arrests and convictions, it makes criminal activities that, by modern standards, are normally innocent, and it places almost unfettered discretion in the hands of the police."[11]

For civil libertarians, the vagueness of vagrancy laws was one reason they were defective and unjust. A second reason was that some of their provisions criminalized status rather than behavior, that is, for *being* something (e.g., unemployed or without a valid address) rather than *doing* something. As such, they were most often used to harass the poor. In 1962, the US Supreme Court invalidated as cruel and unusual punishment a California law that criminalized drug addiction, but it didn't generalize from addiction to status generally.[12] Nonetheless, there was a growing belief within the legal community that status shouldn't be criminalized. Academics were advancing that position in law review articles, and the supreme courts of New York, Nevada and Colorado struck down statutes criminalizing offenses like no visible means of support.[13]

It seemed to us that the Louisiana statute should be declared unconstitutional on both counts—vagueness and wrongly criminalizing status. Regarding the former, among those it deemed vagrant are "Persons who loaf the streets habitually or who frequent the streets habitually at late or unusual hours of the night." Regarding the latter, among the vagrant are "Able-bodied persons without lawful means of support who do not seek employment and take employment when it is available to them."[14]

In 1967, I began trying to find a plaintiff for a court challenge. My quest was frustrating. No one charged with vagrancy called for help, so I looked for arrest notices in the daily newspaper. Usually, however, those arrested were released with credit for time served—five days was the norm—if they had no outstanding warrants. A typical outcome involved the arrest of a man from Houston in August

1967. I went down to the courtroom when he appeared before District Judge Lewis Doherty III. Two days before, he had appeared before Judge Donovan Parker. Then, he had pled innocent and asked for a trial, for which temerity Parker set a trial date for two weeks later. Otherwise, he told reporters, he would have sentenced him to five days but released him for time served, the usual result of guilty pleas in such cases. Given his plea of innocence, I hoped he would allow us to use his case to challenge the statute. I offered to post his $250 bail, but when he told me that he wouldn't stay in town or return to Baton Rouge for a trial, I left. So he changed his plea to guilty, and Doherty sentenced him to time served and ordered his release.

The occasion I remember best concerned a man who had jumped into the Mississippi River and tried to swim out to a cargo ship to seek work. He required rescue and subsequently was booked for vagrancy. His court appearance was scheduled after he had spent two nights in the downtown jail. I reached him shortly before his appearance. The prosecutor then offered to ask the judge to release him for time served if he pled guilty. In good conscience, I couldn't advise the man to reject the plea bargain and contest the law. He wouldn't have been granted bail while the process played out because he wasn't a Baton Rouge resident. So the prosecutor presented the plea bargain to the judge, who approved it. Amazingly, the judge remarked when he did so, "I guess he's been punished enough."

The New Orleans office, happily, had better luck securing plaintiffs to challenge the city vagrancy ordinances and the state statute. In 1967, ACLU cooperating attorney Ben Smith filed *Gordon v. Schiro* on behalf of six plaintiffs. Three of them had been arrested because they stood observing two New Orleans policemen frisking a suspect and refused to move on, a crime under a subsection of the "Idle Persons" ordinance. The fourth was charged for loitering in a department store after being detained and questioned for an hour by a plain clothes detective. The fifth was a US Army private home on leave who was charged with loitering despite showing his ID to the arresting officer. The sixth was a minor charged with "no visible means of support."

*Gordon v. Schiro* made its way through the state courts and got into federal district court in late 1969. The next year, Judge James Comisky ruled the ordinances invalid. That wasn't quite the end of the story. In March 1971, the Fifth Circuit vacated Comisky's ruling, saying that the plaintiffs "had failed to state an appropriate claim for federal intervention." But it noted that the city had repealed the ordinances after Comisky had ruled them unconstitutional.

On February 4, shortly prior to Comisky's ruling and relevant to it, Federal District Judge Alvin Rubin had found sections of the Louisiana statute unconstitutionally vague: "(7) Persons who loaf the streets habitually or who frequent the streets habitually at late or unusual hours of the night, or who loiter around any public place of assembly, without lawful business or reason to be present; or (8) persons found in or near any structure, movable, vessel, or private grounds without being able to account for their lawful presence therein." The case, *Scott v. District Attorney, Jefferson Parish, State of LA.*,[15] originated in the arrest of Nick J. Scott, who was charged with loitering around a rental car agency at the New Orleans airport. Luke Fontana represented him on behalf of the ACLU of Louisiana.

In his opinion, Judge Rubin noted, "Courts in Hawaii and Miami have remarked on the irony of punishing 'loitering' in a resort community whose economy depends on tourists who are invited to enjoy freedom from the workaday necessity to give a good account of themselves. These remarks are also relevant to Louisiana. In fact, New Orleans prides itself on the sobriquet, 'The City That Care Forgot.' The overbreadth of the section making all persons accountable to some (unspecified) inquirer is blatant: the requirement applies to 'Persons found in or near any structure, movable, vessel or private grounds,' a situation it would be difficult for anyone in a settled community to avoid."

Later in the month of Judge Rubin's decision, the New Orleans police used the city's vagrancy ordinances to arrest scores of young people who had come to Mardi Gras and camped in public parks and on the levee. That harassment had been going on for several years. In addition to the generalized police animus against hippies, they wanted to discourage people who weren't going to spend money in hotels and restaurants from competing for space on the streets with paying tourists. But this year, most of the charges were dismissed in municipal court, and on February 25, the city attorney, Alvin Liska, ordered the police to stop making arrests under either the state statute or the city loitering ordinance. The following year, police didn't roust visitors who unrolled their sleeping bags in grassy areas of the French Quarter. One patrolman told a reporter, "If we did, they'd get up and sleep somewhere else. Besides, our vagrancy law has been declared unconstitutional."

Doubtless, in many jurisdictions in Louisiana and in other states, law enforcement continued to use vagrancy laws to arrest "undesirables" even after the U.S. Supreme Court struck down the catch-all provisions of the Florida statute in 1972. Still, it was only a matter of time before this tool of abuse was no longer available to municipal authorities.

*****

I take this opportunity to pay tribute to Ben Smith, mentioned above, because he so richly deserves it. Benjamin Eugene Smith was a nationally prominent civil rights attorney. With Jim Dombrowski, director of the Southern Conference Education Fund (SCEF), he co-founded the ACLU of Louisiana in 1956 and played a major role in dismantling Jim Crow laws in the South. He, Arthur Kinoy, and William Kunstler served as general counsels for the Mississippi Freedom Democratic Party in 1965, and the following year, those three plus Morton Stavis founded the NYC-based Center for Constitutional Rights, which remains a major force in the defense of civil liberties. Ben served a term as president of CCR and one as vice-president of the National Lawyers Guild.

Ben, Jim, and Ben's law associate, Bruce Walzer, were defendants and later plaintiffs in the legal struggle that culminated in the landmark 1965 US Supreme Court decision *Dombrowski v. Pfister* (380 US 479). The case began on October 4, 1963, with a raid by Louisiana State Police, at the direction of the Louisiana Legislature's Joint Committee on Un-American Activities, on Ben's law office and home and the SCEF office. Two days later, the confiscated materials, including SCEF's donor list, were secretly taken to the Mississippi delta office of US Senator James Eastland, who was at the center of a

South-wide strategy of crippling the Civil Rights Movement by prosecuting activists on trumped-up charges that would require time and money to defend against.

All three men were arrested. They had been secretly indicted by a state grand jury under the state's Subversive Activities and Communist Control Law and the Communist Propaganda Control Act. Smith and Walzer were charged with failing to register as agents of the National Lawyers Guild, which the state said had been accused of being a Communist front organization during several Congressional committee hearings. Smith and Dombrowski were charged with failing to register as agents for SCEF, which the state alleged was promoting the overthrow of the state of Louisiana because its members participated in mixed-race meetings and advocated the abolition of the state's segregation laws.

The defendants sued in federal court to enjoin the prosecution. The famous phrase "chilling effect" appears for the first time in *Dombrowski v. Pfister*. Its revolutionary import was that defendants did not have to wait until they were convicted under such laws to attack their constitutionality. The very threat of prosecution for violating such laws was an infringement on the First Amendment rights of free speech, press, and assembly. For the majority, Justice Brennan put it this way: "The mere possibility of erroneous initial application of constitutional standards by a state court *will not ordinarily* constitute irreparable injury warranting federal interference with a good faith prosecution and the adjudication during its course of constitutional defenses. *But equitable relief will be granted to prevent* a substantial loss or impairment of freedoms of expression resulting from prosecution under an excessively broad statute regulating expression" [emphasis added].[16]

I only occasionally saw Ben, mostly at state ACLU board meetings, but I admired him immensely, and my father was pediatrician to the children he had with his second wife, Corinne. They were married from 1965 to 1973. Sadly, Ben in effect drank himself to an early death in 1976. His obituary appeared in the *New York Times*. Beginning that year, annually the state ACLU has presented the Ben Smith Civil Liberties Award.

*****

---

[1] *Shelby County v. Holder*, 570 US 529. Arguing that the data upon which Section 5 of the act was based were outdated the court (which split 5–4) in effect voided the necessity for the originally stipulated states and counties to pre-clear with the U.S. Department of Justice any changes they made regarding voting practices to insure they didn't in effect disenfranchise racial and ethnic minorities. Originally, almost all those jurisdictions were in the deep South. When the act was reauthorized and amended in 1975 and again in 1982, the geography expanded greatly to include protection for Asian Americans, American Indians, Alaskan natives, and "persons of Spanish heritage." The preclearance requirement had been enormously effective in frustrating most schemes to suppress minority voting and the election of minority candidates. Schemes with that intention and effect had a resurgence after *Shelby County v. Holder* ended preclearance. By 2018, nearly one thousand polling places had been closed in the United States, many of them in predominantly African-American counties. There have been purges of voter rolls, curtailment of opportunities for early voting, and imposition of strict voter ID laws. Unlike the original attempts at subversion, these have been carried out, not by Whites but by Republicans, who have now become an overwhelmingly White political party.

2  *Los Angeles Times*, May 25, 1990. A stringer for the Times Wire Services wrote the story, which was about a storytelling session three of the early Black state legislators held on the steps of the state capitol as part of Louisiana Open House 1990, a tourism promotion put on by the state.

3  Blacks in New Orleans didn't face the same challenge. The city's Home Rule Charter of 1954, which remained unchanged after the Voting Rights Act passed, provided for a mayor-council form of government. The council is composed of seven members, five of whom are elected from single-member districts and two at large.

4  For a comprehensive discussion of the legal history, see Abigail Thernstrom, "Redistricting, Race, and the Voting Rights Act." National Affairs, Spring 2010.

5  *White v. Regester*, 412 US 755 (1973).

6  See Chapter 6 on school integration, note 5, for an explanation of the three large all-Black geographical areas of the city.

7  From 1982 to 1994, Reverend Jemison was president of the National Baptist Convention, USA, the country's largest African-American religious organization. His base was Mt. Zion First Baptist Church in Baton Rouge, to which he was called as minister in 1949. In 1953, he led a campaign to desegregate the public buses in Baton Rouge, which included a boycott with a free-ride network. After two weeks, a compromise was reached that didn't end segregation, which was mandated by state law but assured that Black riders would have access on a first-come first-served basis to all but the front two seats. Jemison's management of the boycott became a model for the far more well-known Montgomery bus boycott two years later. For a full account, see Susan Altman's article in The Encyclopedia of African-American Heritage, New York: Facts on File, Inc., 1997.

8  See Chapter 9.

[9] *Hair: The American Tribal Love-Rock Musical,* with book and lyrics by Gerome Ragni and James Rado and music by Galt MacDermot, opened off Broadway in October 1967. A cast album was released in 1967. It opened on Broadway in April 1968 and ran for 1,750 performances.

[10] Karr v. Schmidt, 401 US 1201 (1971). Explaining the refusal to hear the case, Justice Hugo Black wrote, "I refuse to hold for myself that the federal courts have constitutional power to interfere in this way with the public school system operated by the States. And I furthermore refuse to predict that our Court will hold they have such power. It is true that we have held that this Court does have power under the Fourteenth Amendment to bar state public schools from discriminating against Negro students on account of their race but we did so by virtue of a direct, positive command in the Fourteenth Amendment, which, like the other Civil War Amendments, was primarily designed to outlaw racial discrimination by the States. There is no such direct, positive command about local school rules with reference to the length of hair state school students must have. And I cannot now predict this Court will hold that the more or less vague terms of either the Due Process or Equal Protection Clause have robbed the States of their traditionally recognized power to run their school systems in accordance with their own best judgment as to the appropriate length of hair for students."

[11] *Papachristou v. City of Jacksonville,* 405 US 156 (1972). *Papachristou* consolidated the appeals of eight convictions stemming from five separate actions by Jacksonville police. A portion of the facts presented to the court are worth citing to illustrate the ways vagrancy statutes habitually were used.

    Margaret Papachristou and Betty Calloway were White females. Eugene Eddie Melton and Leonard Johnson were black males. Papachristou was enrolled in a job-training program sponsored by the State Employment Service at Florida Junior

College in Jacksonville. Calloway was a typing and shorthand teacher at a state mental institution located near Jacksonville. She was the owner of the automobile in which the four defendants were arrested. Melton was a Vietnam war veteran who had been released from the navy after nine months in a veterans' hospital. On the date of his arrest, he was a part-time computer helper while attending college as a full-time student in Jacksonville. Johnson was a tow-motor operator in a grocery chain warehouse and was a lifelong resident of Jacksonville.

At the time of their arrest, the four of them were riding in Calloway's car on the main thoroughfare in Jacksonville. They had left a restaurant owned by Johnson's uncle where they had eaten and were on their way to a nightclub. The arresting officers denied that the racial mixture in the car played any part in the decision to make the arrest. The arrest, they said, was made because the defendants had stopped near a used-car lot which had been broken into several times. There was, however, no evidence of any breaking and entering on the night in question. Of these four charged with "prowling by auto," none had been previously arrested except Papachristou, who had once been convicted of a municipal offense.

Jimmy Lee Smith and Milton Henry were arrested between 9:00 and 10:00 a.m. on a weekday in downtown Jacksonville while waiting for a friend who was to lend them a car so they could apply for a job at a produce company. Smith was a part-time produce worker and part-time organizer for a Negro political group. He had a common-law wife and three children supported by him and his wife. He had been arrested several times but convicted only once. Henry was an eighteen-year-old high school student with no previous record of arrest. That morning was cold and Smith had no jacket, so they went briefly into a dry cleaning shop to wait but left when requested to do so. They thereafter walked back and forth two or three times over a two-block stretch looking for their friend. The store owners, who apparently were wary of Smith and his companion, summoned two police officers who searched the men and found neither had a weapon. But they were arrested because the officers said they had no identification and because the officers did not believe their story.

Henry Heath and a codefendant were arrested for "loitering" and for being a "common thief." Both were residents of Jacksonville; Heath had lived there all his life and was employed at an automobile body shop. He had previously been arrested, but his codefendant had no arrest record. Heath and his companion were arrested when they drove up to a residence shared by Heath's girlfriend and some other young women. Some police officers were already there in the process of arresting another man. When Heath and his companion started backing out of the driveway, the officers signaled to them to stop and asked them to get out of the car, which they did. They and the automobile were searched. Although no contraband or incriminating evidence was found, they were both arrested, Heath being charged with being a "common thief" because he was reputed to be a thief. The codefendant was charged with "loitering" because he was standing in the driveway, an act which the officers admitted was done only at their command.

[12] *Robinson v. California*, 370 US 660 (1962).

[13] For a review of the pertinent case law through 1968 as well as other law review articles on vagrancy, see Harry M. Zimmerman Jr., "Louisiana Vagrancy Law—Constitutionally Sound," 29 *Louisiana Law Review* (1969). It's hard to account for the title the editors of the law review put on the title page of the article. The heading of the text itself says "Constitutionally Unsound," and that is how Zimmerman deemed several of the law's provisions.

[14] Zimmerman (*supra*) analyzes the Louisiana statute in detail.

[15] 309 F. Supp. 833 (E. D. La. 1970).

[16] In *Rights on Trial* (Harvard University Press, 1983), Arthur Kinoy gives an extended account of *Dombrowski v. Pfister.* When the arrests were made, Kinoy and Kunstler were in New Orleans for a conference of the Lawyers Guild Committee to Assist Southern Lawyers that had been organized by the ACLU of Louisiana and the Louis A. Martinet Society, an association of New Orleans's Black lawyers. Kinoy was one of the two attorneys who argued the case before the US Supreme Court. *Rights on Trial* is a firsthand account of many of the great struggles for freedom and justice starting shortly after World War II. It is dedicated to four people, among them Ben, Jim Dombrowski, and Fannie Lou Hamer of the Mississippi Freedom Democratic Party.

I was fortunate enough to become acquainted with Arthur when I was executive director of New Jersey SANE/ Freeze from 1987–1990. It was headquartered in Montclair, where Arthur lived. He was teaching at the Rutgers Law School and still involved in multiple struggles. I treasure the inscription he wrote on the flyleaf of the copy of *Rights on Trial* he gave me:

To Herb,

> With deep respect and affection to a brother in the long struggles for the rights of the people—for their fundamental liberties—for their freedom—and for their power. We are together.

—Arthur Kinoy, April 1990

# CHAPTER 9

## Things Turn Ugly

After the two assassinations in 1968—Robert Kennedy's following Martin Luther King's by barely two months—the mood of the country seemed to sour. The war had ruined everything. It ruptured the crucial alliance between the national administration and the Civil Rights Movement; it doomed Lyndon Johnson's War on Poverty; it ended youthful dreams of a transformed consciousness; and it paved the way for Richard Nixon.

The event that, for me, best represents the turning point occurred the year before. It was King's speech at Riverside Church in New York City on April 4, 1967. Titled "Beyond Vietnam: A Time to Break Silence," in it he endorsed the call of the National Emergency Committee of Clergy and Laymen Concerned about Vietnam for an end to the war and agreed to be its co-chair. He did so against the advice of other leaders of the Civil Rights Movement, knowing as well as they that it would mean a decisive break with the Johnson Administration. But King had a much clearer understanding than they that the struggle for equal rights now had to be a struggle for economic justice, and the war was an insurmountable stumbling block.

In the Riverside speech, King put it this way: "A few years ago…it seemed as if there was a real promise of hope for the poor, both black and white, through the poverty program. There were experiments, hopes, new beginnings. Then came the buildup in Vietnam, and I watched this program broken and eviscerated as if it were some idle political plaything of a society gone mad on war. And I knew that America would never invest the necessary funds or energies in rehabilitation of its poor so long as adventures like Vietnam continued to draw men and skills and money like some demonic, destructive suction tube."

One of the several reasons King gave for his decision to break silence about the war was that its terrible violence contravened his efforts to persuade angry Blacks in cities outside the South to walk the path of nonviolence. According to the report of the President's National Advisory Commission on Civil Disorders (widely known as the Kerner Commission because it was chaired by Illinois Gov. Otto Kerner), from 1965 through 1967, there had been more than 150 riots or major disturbances, the deadliest of them in Los Angeles, Detroit, and Newark, New Jersey. Speaking of his experience during those three years, King said, "As I have walked among the desperate, rejected, and angry young men, I have told them that Molotov cocktails and rifles would not solve their problems. I have tried to offer them my deepest compassion while maintaining my conviction that social change comes most meaningfully through nonviolent action. But they asked, and rightly so, 'What about Vietnam?' They asked if our own nation

wasn't using massive doses of violence to solve its problems, to bring about the changes it wanted. Their questions
hit home, and I knew that I could never again raise my
voice against the violence of the oppressed in the ghettos
without having first spoken clearly to the greatest purveyor
of violence in the world today: my own government."

Johnson's response to the widespread rioting that
immediately followed King's assassination was a mixed
one. On the one hand, he wasn't surprised. According to
George Christian, his press secretary, he said, "What did
you expect? I don't know why we're so surprised. When
you put your foot on a man's neck and hold him down for
three hundred years, and then you let him up, what's he
going to do? He's going to knock your block off."[1] The turbulence allowed him to push through Congress his long-
stalled Fair Housing legislation as part of the 1968 Civil
Rights Act.

On the other hand, Johnson was increasingly toler-
ant of force to suppress dissent. In advance of the Poor
People's Campaign's arrival in Washington, which began on
May 12 with a speech by Coretta Scott King, he activated
twenty thousand US Army soldiers, who were instructed
to prepare for a military occupation of the capital should
the Campaign turn violent. And he remained silent as
Chicago Mayor Richard Daley, his political ally at the 1968
Democratic National Convention in rejecting a peace plank
in the party platform and securing the presidential nomina-
tion for Vice-President Hubert Humphrey, unleashed city
police and National Guardsmen on the thousands of young
people who had come to the 1968 Democratic National
Convention to persuade the delegates to reject the war.

After the Poor People's Campaign was evicted from its "Resurrection City" on the National Mall on June 24, 1968, it was no longer possible to identify a Civil Rights Movement. The Anti-War Movement kept together longer. The Moratorium to End the War in Vietnam was held worldwide on October 15, 1969,[2] followed by a massive demonstration in Washington a month later. But when Nixon intensified the violence even while he slowly drew down the troops, that movement also fractured organizationally and ideologically. Monopolizing the headlines were groups that fed on fantasies of violent revolution. The threat they posed to "law and order," the reactionary rallying cry that helped propel Nixon to the White House, was used to justify the extensive use that federal and local law enforcement made of undercover spies, *agents provocateurs* and trumped-up prosecutions. These tactics took a heavy toll on legitimate dissent.

*****

I can't remember any large-scale turbulence in Baton Rouge until city police fatally shot in the back two unarmed Black kids within three weeks of each other in July 1969. The only similar event after I had come to Baton Rouge had occurred almost two years before, and the contrast was notable. Governor John McKeithen had called out the National Guard and state police to help maintain order when simultaneous rallies, one by Black activists demanding more state hiring of Black workers and the other by Klansmen intent on disruption, were held on Saturday, August 19, 1967, and again on Sunday, August 20. That weekend, law enforcement shielded Blacks from White violence and acted with restraint when a few Black youths started some small fires in the Eden Park area. No one was injured.[3]

But this time, anger mounted after a parish grand jury refused to indict Officer Luther Coates for killing Lionel Hughes and after Baton Rouge Police Chief Eddie O. Bauer reneged on his promise to suspend Officer Ray Breaux pending grand jury action on his killing of James Oliney Jr.[4] Rioting began after a rally on Thursday, July 31 organized by state and local NAACP leaders and attended by about six hundred people. A young Black man named Jerry Johnson gave an incendiary speech, for which he was arrested on the charge of inciting a riot, deemed a felony by a recently-passed anti-riot law. Shortly after the rally, there were physical attacks on White people and stoning of their cars.

Mayor-President W. W. "Woody" Dumas imposed a curfew at 7:30 that evening. A number of fires, three of them serious, broke out after dark mainly in Black neighborhoods. More than twenty Blacks had been arrested by midnight, most for violating the curfew. The next morning Governor McKeithen sent in some 700 National Guardsmen and 250 state police to help patrol the streets. There was no subsequent renewal of the rioting.

Within a few days, I attended a community meeting with Chief Bauer. As I recall, I was the only White person there. Feelings among the Black participants were running high. Even Gus Young, a longtime and generally compliant community leader whose political base was in Eden Park, threatened Bauer with more violence if the shootings didn't stop. I spoke briefly, telling Bauer that the rioting was justified given that neither he nor Sargent Pitcher, the district attorney, had indicated that they would put a stop to the killings.

The Baton Rouge Council on Human Relations asked the US Department of Justice to send federal marshals "to restrain the Baton Rouge Police from acts of police brutality." Against my better judgment, the local ACLU chapter sent a similar request to the FBI. Neither organization got a reply. The Nixon-Mitchell Justice Department was a far cry from the Johnson-Clark department. At most, public announcement of these calls may have added some pressure on Dumas and Bauer.

The Legal Aid Society took a more aggressive action. On August 4, it filed a suit in federal court on behalf of the next of kin of Hughes, Oliney, and a fifteen-year-old Black male, Melvin Parmer, killed by police two years before. It asked the court to enjoin the conduct of the Baton Rouge police to assure "availability of police protection and treatment by police in a manner which does not discriminate on the basis of race and color." Named as defendants were the mayor, every member of the city-parish council, the police chief and Bryan Clemmons, the sheriff. The most inflammatory of the many abuses cited in the suit was "acts of solicitation and exposure of genital parts to young black females."

Judge E. Gordon West refused to issue a restraining order and indicated that he didn't want the suit tried because it might inflame racial tensions. It dragged on until 1973, when an agreement was reached that included almost none of the remedies originally sought. The main concession the defendants made was to immediately suspend any officer who shot a suspect pending an investigation and a grand jury determination. What wasn't conceded was a revision of the rule governing police use of deadly force, forbidding it except to defend their lives or prevent imminent bodily harm to themselves or others.

The unintended result of the suit was the reining in of the young lawyers who had come to work for the Legal Aid Society so they could promote social change. Capital Area United Givers, pressed by several of its large donors, told Legal Aid that it must never file such suits again if it wanted to retain United Givers funding. The threat worked. Legal Aid reverted to its traditional function of providing personal legal services to indigent individuals.

What happened to Legal Aid locally was part of a national pattern. Legal aid offices associated with the Office of Economic Opportunity (OEO) were the brightest spot of the War on Poverty. In such areas as public housing and welfare rights, they didn't just provide services to poor people, they empowered them, which upset entrenched political and economic interests. California Rural Legal Assistance was especially proactive, joining clients like farmworkers on picket lines and advocating for them at the state legislature as well as in the courts. Ronald Reagan, governor at the time, tried hard to get OEO to cut off its funding but failed.

It was Congress that curtailed the ability of OEO-funded legal services to promote social change. The restrictions were codified in the 1974 Legal Services Corporation Act. In 1972, when such restrictions were first proposed, I wrote in my capacity as president of the state ACLU to Louisiana's US Senator Russell Long, urging him to oppose any curtailment of legal services activities. In his response, he told me that his idea of legal services was quite different than mine. He believed that its proper function was to help poor people file for bankruptcies and get divorces. I wondered to myself what Huey P. Long, that great champion of the poor, would have thought of his son.

On August 13, Sargent Pitcher guided the grand jury to find Officer Breaux innocent of any wrongdoing in his killing of Oliney. At the same time, he got a felony indictment against Emmitt Douglas, president of state NAACP, for inciting a riot when Douglas spoke after Jerry Johnson at the rally. That bogus prosecution was one of several Pitcher used to disrupt social change activities by requiring organizations to devote time and resources to defend against the charges.

Judge West refused to halt the prosecutions of Johnson and Douglas, holding that the anti-riot act didn't create a "chilling effect" on First Amendment exercise (see my discussion of *Dombrowski v. Pfister* near the end of the previous chapter). So in separate trials in February 1971, both Johnson and Douglas were found guilty of misdemeanors. In June, Judge Elmo Lear sentenced Johnson to six months in jail and Douglas to a $350 fine and three months in jail suspended. He released both men on bail pending their appeals. In June 1973, the Louisiana Supreme Court vacated Douglas' conviction because it determined that no evidence was presented at trial that he had urged the audience to riot. Eventually, Judge Lear reduced Johnson's jail sentence to a fine, in part to deny him grounds to challenge the constitutionality of the state anti-riot statute.

Later that year, Baton Rouge police shot in the back and killed another young Black man, Wilbur Triche, under suspicious circumstances. A new police chief, Rudolph Ratcliffe, suspended the three officers involved. By this time, Ossie Brown had replaced Sargent Pitcher as district attorney. There were no civil disturbances this time. That may have been, in part, because of the suspensions and Brown's credibility with the Black community. Brown presented the case to a grand jury the following January, which cleared the officers, who were then reinstated. But the city-parish council, on which Blacks now held four of the twelve seats, mandated a change of policy governing police use of deadly force, at last restricting it to situations when life or bodily harm was imminently threatened. After that change went into effect, I cannot remember another problematic police killing until 1984.[5]

Pitcher's replacement by Brown as district attorney marked a major step forward for race relations and civil liberties in the parish. The election was held in 1972. Our ACLU chapter persistently criticized Pitcher, although we couldn't call for his defeat. I personally supported Frank Foil, who was Pitcher's other opponent. Brown had significant Black support, largely because two years earlier, he had successfully defended Louisiana native Army Staff Sergeant David Mitchell, a squad leader under Lt. William Calley's command, who was tried in a military court at Fort Hood, Texas in connection with the My Lai Massacre. In the primary, Pitcher finished third after Brown and Foil. Brown then won the runoff and served through 1984. Foil later became a state district judge.

\*\*\*\*\*

The first indication we had that the Baton Rouge police department was running an undercover operation on the LSU campus was in March 1969, when eighteen students—thirteen from LSU, five from Southern—were arrested while they were supporting a strike at the Acme Brick Company. A student named Charles Spillers was among them, but the arresting officers separated him from the others and he wasn't charged. Capt. Leroy Watson, head of the Intelligence Division, later identified him as a police agent. Spillers was also sharing information he gathered with the Louisiana Joint Legislative Committee on Un-American Activities.

Nationally, many antiwar activists had begun to advocate support for workers' struggles as a way of broadening the movement and softening the widespread hostility of blue-collar Americans to anti-war protests and the college students at its fore. That was one reason for the decision by the Student Liberal Federation (SLF) at LSU to join striking workers at Acme. Another was that all forty-seven of the strikers were Black. Jodie Bibbins, past president of the Black Student Union at Southern, had come to LSU and asked that LSU students join his group's support of the strikers. The next day, the action at the plant took place.

The charges were disturbing the peace and aggravated obstruction of a highway, the latter a felony. DA Sargent Pitcher's pretext for bringing so serious a charge was that the students had piled up tree stumps and crossties in the driveway to prevent scabs from driving trucks in and out of the plant. It was Spillers who began doing that and urging others to follow suit, which strongly suggested that he had been prompted to set the students up. Whether that was true, the charge was unwarranted. The statute was designed to prevent actions that endangered life, such as strewing tacks on a thoroughfare. In this case, there was no thoroughfare and no potential for physical harm.

Bond for the students was set at $1,000, which I publicly protested as unwarranted given the defendants' status in the community and the nature of their action. Louis Simpson, the father of one defendant, was a professor in my department. He asked me to help his son. I arranged for his legal representation. Before the trial in June 1970, Pitcher had dropped charges against two of the defendants, and one had pled guilty, paid a $200 fine and spent ninety days in jail. That plea was a mistake because at Simpson's trial Judge Donovan Parker agreed with his attorney that the statute was "unconstitutionally vague and overbroad" and dismissed the charge. He subsequently did the same for the other defendants.

After Spillers's exposure as an undercover agent, Captain Watson, his handler, justified planting an informant on campus by saying he was simply trying to anticipate any trouble the formation of an SDS chapter might cause. Spillers was assigned to feel out "the more militant" members of the SLF and the Martin Luther King Action Movement who might form an SDS chapter. He didn't mention Spillers' actions as an *agent provocateur*. Spillers left LSU but continued to work for the police department as an undercover narcotics agent. He was also the department's liaison to another of its agents on campus, Gus Taboney.

Taboney worked undercover at LSU for five years before he was outed in 1974. At that time, he was a senior in the law school, financial vice-president of the Student

Government Association, and a candidate for SGA president. He had also been a member of the SDS chapter that did form shortly after the episode at the Acme Brick Company but which had little support and quickly died out. He then helped form the Progressive Student Alliance, successor to the SLF, and became its president.

It was the Reveille, LSU's student newspaper, that disclosed on March 13, 1974, that Taboney was a police agent. The week before, Spillers had obtained a warrant to search the residence of three LSU students, among them John Porterfield, one of Taboney's opponents in the race for SGA president. Porterfield wasn't home at the time, but his two roommates were arrested because the police allegedly found a half ounce of pot on the premises. A Reveille reporter looking into Spillers's duties discovered his connection with Taboney, who confirmed that he was an agent but denied any knowledge of the search.

A student whom I knew who was active in the Progressive Student Alliance came to my office quite distraught over the revelation. He told me that Taboney had presented himself as the most radical member of the group and had tried to get them to engage in illegal activities. He felt a deep sense of betrayal. Destroying trust was one of the intended consequences of planting spies and *agents provocateurs* in such organizations. It worked.

The university administration said it was shocked at the revelation. Chancellor Cecil Taylor said his office would investigate the "implications" of Taboney's dual status as a student government officeholder and an informant. Nothing came of that. Taboney was finished as a campus leader, and apparently the administration was finished with the issue. The ACLU chapter, then led by Paul Grosser, who taught in the Political Science Department, criticized the administration's failure to take a stand against police informants on campus. It called for the expulsion of students who worked undercover, contending that their presence was inimical to an atmosphere of "free and open discussion and inquiry." Shortly before, the California Supreme Court had ruled that the routine stationing of paid informants on public campuses violated the state constitution's guarantee of the right of privacy. Louisiana, however, was not California.

*****

The trouble stirred up by an informant and *agent provo-cateur* the police department had placed among community activists in Scotlandville, the Black section of the city where Southern University is located, was uglier than the events at LSU. It resulted in the arrests of three young men for plotting to assassinate the mayor of Baton Rouge and the police chief of the city of Plaquemine in Iberville Parish.

James Lee "Tiny Tim" Moore, the informant, was uglier too. He had killed an unarmed man in a bar fight in 1965, but the jury acquitted him after police testified that he was an informant. Two months after the alleged assassination attempt, Moore killed another man in a bar fight. This time, he wasn't even indicted. Apparently, Captain Watson and Sargent Pitcher put a high value on his services.

Alphonse Snedecor, twenty-two, was arrested on Friday, March 20, 1970, at 10:45 a.m. as he stood with a rifle in tall grass beside the Illinois Central railroad track along the route Mayor Dumas usually drove from his home in Baker to City Hall in downtown Baton Rouge. Later that day, police executed arrest warrants for Frank Stewart and Wade Hudson Jr., and searched the residence they shared. Bail was set for all three arrestees at $100,000. Named in the case but not arrested was Jodie Bibbins, twenty-eight, former head of the Black Student Union at Southern. Like Bibbins, Stewart and Hudson, twenty-four and twenty-three respectively, were activists. Stewart, a Southern University graduate, had spent two years with the Peace Corps in Nigeria. On his return, with Hudson he organized SOUL—Society for Opportunity, Unity, and Leadership. Stewart and Hudson were employed by VISTA—Volunteers in Service to America—when they were arrested.

Snedecor was also a member of SOUL, but he was a psychologically troubled man. He had been court martialed and given an administrative discharge from the US army. And he had killed a man named David Huddleston in 1969, although he was not tried and convicted for that crime until 1973. In January 1976, District Attorney Ossie Brown dismissed the charges against Snedecor stemming from the alleged assassination plot, stating that a lunacy commission had found that Snedecor was a paranoid schizophrenic at the time of the incident. By then, Snedecor was in the state penitentiary at Angola serving a life sentence for the murder of Huddleston.

The afternoon of the arrests, Pitcher held a news conference in his office. He said that the arrests stemmed from an investigation that "began about a week ago when the city police intelligence division picked up information" about the conspiracy. He said that the suspects were then kept under surveillance around the clock until "an overt act was committed." Pitcher didn't divulge how the police had "picked up" their information. Five days later, however, when the documents filed with the court to obtain the arrest and search warrants were made public, they revealed that "police used a confidential informant." There were also photographs of Snedecor and the informant purchasing the rifle at Gibson's, a store on Airline Highway, on the morning of the twentieth. Thus, Moore's identity became known.

Snedecor had come to Stewart's apartment with Moore on Monday of that week and introduced Moore to Stewart. On that occasion, Stewart said, Moore asked him who he wanted to kill, which Stewart thought was a crazy thing to ask someone he had just met. Foolishly, Stewart agreed to go target shooting with the other two in Moore's car. On the way back, Moore again spoke of killing White people. He drove them by the spot where the arrest was made four days later, which was why the police had a photograph of Stewart at the site. When Stewart got home, he told Hudson not to let Moore ever come into the apartment again. Snedecor came over the following day and told Stewart that Moore was a police informant and that he was just stringing Moore along. It's hard to understand, though, why he went with Moore that morning.

Pitcher had Snedecor and Stewart indicted for attempted murder. Not Hudson, though, who was named as a material witness and released on a $5,000 bond. Ben Smith[6] agreed to represent Stewart. He filed a $1 million suit in federal district court against Pitcher, Moore, and Watson, and asked Judge West to set aside the bail and to stay the prosecution against Stewart. Judge West did set aside the bail, calling it "unreasonable and improper and unconstitutional," and Stewart was released on August 11 after five months behind bars. But West refused to issue a temporary injunction to stop the prosecution from going forward.

But Pitcher never did prosecute Stewart or Snedecor. Stewart's case dragged out in the federal courts. West ruled in in November 1970 against a permanent injunction. Smith appealed to the Fifth Circuit, which sent the case back to West and required him to hold a hearing to determine if the prosecution was launched in bad faith. That hearing was held on December 16, 1971, partly behind closed doors. West refused to support the claim that the episode was a police plot to entrap Black activists. He disregarded the role Moore played, including purchasing the rifle, and dismissed as unproved the testimony of witnesses, including Stewart, about the damage the arrests and pending prosecution had caused to SOUL, as well as other police harassment of SOUL leaders. West also held two newsmen in contempt and fined them each $300 for violating his order not to publish details of the open hearing.[7]

Because of his indictment and conviction for killing Huddleston, Snedecor never was released from custody. Stewart, however, was able to carry on his life, including attending the University of Massachusetts for graduate work. After Pitcher was voted out of office, Ossie Brown inherited the case. In 1974, Brown said he would set a trial date, but he never did. Instead, and at last, in January 1976, he dismissed the charges against both defendants. What he said regarding Stewart on that occasion was puzzling: "With reference to defendant Stewart, I am honoring in this action a commitment made by the district attorney's office prior to my becoming district attorney. I do not feel at liberty to reveal the details of this commitment nor to pass judgment on it except to say it involved the utilization of Stewart in highly confidential governmental work."

Edward Deevy, who was in charge of the VISTA office when Stewart and Hudson worked there, had organized a fundraising effort for the three men shortly after their arrests. I went to a gathering at his apartment; Ben Smith was there as well. But after Stewart was released, Deevy told me that Stewart had been working for the police. He didn't tell me how he had learned about it or when Stewart had started or what he was doing.

I had no way of evaluating that accusation, but Brown's cryptic remarks when he dismissed the charge lent credence to Deevy's claim. If Stewart cooperated with Pitcher in some way, it must have been after his arrest. It seems improbable that Pitcher would have kept him in jail for five months had Stewart been working with the police before the event. That hadn't been the way he treated Spillers when the arrests were made at Acme Brick or Moore in this case. I doubt that the truth of this matter will ever become public knowledge. What is certain, though, is that Pitcher and Watson once again had achieved their objective of disrupting social change activity in the city.

\*\*\*\*\*

Neither Pitcher nor the police were the immediate cause of the bloodiest racial confrontation that occurred while I lived in Baton Rouge. The clash between a group of Black Muslims and the city police and sheriff's deputies on January 10, 1972, left two deputies and two Muslims dead. A third Muslim died in hospital seventeen days later, and TV newsman Bob Johnson sustained head injuries so severe that he was permanently impaired.

Some key questions remain unanswered. It's doubtful that these Muslims were in good standing with the Nation of Islam. After the episode, Elijah Muhammed said that they weren't on the registry, and the local Nation of Islam minister said no member of the group had contacted him when they came to town. They were certainly Black Muslims, though. They dressed in the standard black suits and bowties, manifested the same rigorous discipline, and referred to Whites as "white devils." When they were in parish prison awaiting trial, they requested ACLU help because they weren't allowed access to the Koran. I arranged for our staff attorney in New Orleans to represent them. We successfully asserted their right to the Koran but not to uncensored mail. We didn't represent them against charges, however, since the prosecution didn't *prima facie* violate their constitutional rights. Over their eight years of trials and appeals, the defendants were represented by a number of attorneys, most prominently Murphy Bell, who had been the leading Black attorney in Baton Rouge since the 1950s.

It's also unclear why the Muslims had come to Baton Rouge. The license plates of their vehicles were California and Illinois. There were some indications that they were seeking a home base. The day after the fatal encounter, the *Tampa Times* ran a story reporting that at least one of the men involved had been among a group of four who had come to Tampa in late December. Among the information the *Times* reporters had gathered was that the group had inquired about purchasing a large house to use as a headquarters, but that police who called on them at the motel where they stayed had convinced them that Tampa wasn't the right community. A Baton Rouge resident named Samuel Jenkins, who was in the Masonic Building on North Boulevard when several of the group came in to rent meeting space for the night of January 7, said that when he asked where their headquarters were, he was told they were considering establishing it in Baton Rouge.

All of the group were under thirty, most under twenty-five. When they checked into the White House Inn Hotel on January 4, David McKinney signed the register and put under his name, "The Young Muslims."[8] It's most likely that after they had received Nation of Islam training, they had been unable to stay and were trying to establish their own parallel organization without any clear vision of the future or whether they even had a future. Several witnesses to the clash, including Charles Granger, who was working for the local anti-poverty agency, reported hearing the men say they were prepared to die. Certainly, their behavior on January 10 courted death.

Which is not to say that they began the violent encounter with city police and sheriff deputies. The most critical of the unanswered questions were whether the Muslims had any firearms and who starting the shooting. It was the inability of the district attorney—first Pitcher, then Ossie

Brown—to make a convincing case that the Muslims were armed or ever pulled a trigger that frustrated their effort to convict anyone of murder. They had to settle for "inciting a riot" convictions.

The verifiable beginning of the fatal confrontation was on December 30, when three Muslims were arrested for soliciting money without a license in the downtown business district. Those three and at least one other man, Robert Barber, had checked into the Bellemont Hotel on December 29. The next day, James Kolter, manager of the city's Better Business Bureau, received a call from business owners on Third Street and had gone there to investigate. He spoke to one of the Muslims, Eugene Varnado, who said the fundraising was for an arts and cultural center in Chicago. After Varnado refused Kolter's request that he come to the BBB office and talk further about the matter, Kolter called the police. They were charged with soliciting without a license, and a $5,000 bond was set for each of the three, which they couldn't make.

Had not so high a bond been set for so minor a charge, had the men just been asked to leave town in return for dropping the charge, the terrible events of January 10 probably would have never occurred. That is what defense attorneys pointed out in the two trials—the first one in April 1973, the second in June 1976 after the first verdict was set aside by the Louisiana Supreme Court.[9]

That the three men were being held in jail didn't become public knowledge for a long time. The police apparently told the news media that they had been released without charge. At least that's what was reported in a lengthy story the *Advocate* ran the Sunday after the confrontation. Further, it reported that Captain Watson said he had sent three officers to the Bellemont Hotel, who told the men staying there that they needed to stop soliciting and received a promise that they would.

Whoever was left of the original group checked out on January 1. Where they went is unknown, but they returned with a much larger group on Thursday, January 4—fourteen men and two women checked into the White House Inn Hotel near the state capitol. They held a public meeting the next night on the roof of the Masonic Building in the 1300 block of North Boulevard, which then housed the Temple Theater. According to Black businessman Frank Millican, the meeting was sparsely attended, mostly by young men, and was brief. The flyer for the meeting promised "a right now change," and Millican said that one of the Muslims said the group had come "to deliver the city back to the black people." He said people should come back on Monday at noon to see how they would do it.

Most of the Muslims—not all—showed up by the theater Monday before 10:00 a.m. Rumors had spread that there was to be a confrontation, and a sizable crowd was gathering. Police sent several plainclothes officers but none in uniform. At ten, another meeting was held inside the building. Three reporters for WBRZ TV—Maurice Cockerham, Bob Johnson and Henry Baptiste—were on the scene by noon. Two doors from the Masonic building was the office of Reed Canada, who owned an advertising business and was a community leader. The three reporters went there to find out what he knew about the gathering. While they were talking, a Cadillac and a Toyota, two of the cars belonging to the group, were pulled across North Boulevard, blocking traffic. One Muslim, Samuel Upton, climbed atop the Cadillac and began speaking to the crowd, which reportedly numbered between two hundred and three hundred people.

When the three newsmen walked out of Canada's office to observe, some Blacks told them to leave. They turned and began to walk away but were attacked. Johnson was struck on the head and was bleeding badly when he tried to run. Then he was hit by a thrown bottle and went down. Cockerham fled into an alley and called the police, urging them to get to the scene quickly. Baptiste, who had fled unscathed, went back for Johnson, got him into his (Baptiste's) car, and drove him to Our Lady of the Lake Hospital, which at that time was nearby. None of the Muslims was identified as Johnson's assailant, and no one was ever prosecuted for assaulting him.

Uniformed police and sheriff's deputies began arriving at about 12:45. The Muslims had formed a line in front of the Toyota and stood there quietly. Crowds lined both sides of the street. A police wrecker arrived. On a signal by Upton, the Muslims stepped away and reformed their line in front of the Cadillac. The Toyota was towed away. The deputies, led by Major Fred Sliman, faced the Muslims. City police, led by Chief Bauer, formed behind the Muslims. Sliman and Bob Bleiden of the Sheriff's Department walked toward the line, and Police Major Jim Dumigan moved through the line from the back and joined them. Sliman said that they had to allow the Cadillac to be towed so the street could clear. Upton replied defiantly. What followed was two minutes of chaotic violence. Statements

about what occurred from start to finish were character-
ized by uncertainty and inconsistency.

Sliman and some Black witnesses said that one of
the Muslims struck Dumigan without warning. Other
Black witnesses said that Dumigan was struck only when
he tried to move through the line again. Sliman then tried
to breach the line and was struck. A policeman moved in
swinging his billy club. Then a shot was fired. Sliman and
Granger said it came from a vacant lot along the street.
Deputy Bryan Clemmons Jr., son of the sheriff, gave an
entirely different account. He said that he saw one of the
Muslims pull a chrome-plated .38 revolver from his coat, so
Clemmons, who had a shotgun loaded with teargas, fired at
him. Clemmons went on to say that almost simultaneously,
some other officer shot the same man with buckshot and
he fell. Then shots started coming from several directions.
Canada later said, "People were falling like flies, like when
we went into Omaha Beach."[10]

When the firing stopped, Deputies Ralph Hancock and
DeWayne Wilder and Muslims Thomas Davis and Upton
lay dead. More than thirty persons, including five officers
and five Muslims, were wounded or injured. One of the
wounded Muslims, Lonnie X (Larry Mobley), died seventeen days later. Twenty people were arrested. Eight were
charged with murder; a ninth was added later after being
released from hospital. Of those, eight were Muslims from
out of town, and Robert Eames was a Baton Rouge resident caught up in the melee. Bail was set at $500,000. A cur-
few was imposed on the city, and seven hundred National
Guardsmen were called in to patrol the streets. That lasted
three nights. Dozens of Blacks were arrested for curfew

violations, but the city stayed calm. Outrageously, bail was set for curfew violators at $25,000 but was later drastically reduced.

Intent on making the murder charge stick, both the district attorney and various law enforcement spokespersons claimed that the Muslims had weapons. That claim was never corroborated. Police recovered no guns at the scene other than those belonging to police. Another claim was that the Muslims grabbed guns from officers and used them. That claim too remained unsubstantiated. Sheriff Detective Bleiden insisted, "Anybody who tells you they can remember what happened after the shooting started is lying." It's highly likely that all the bullets came from law enforcement, who were shooting into the skirmish line from both the front and back.

What wasn't in doubt was that the Muslims provoked a confrontation. If their motive was to demonstrate to onlookers an utter lack of fear of the police, they succeeded. One young Black man who was at the scene told a reporter, "I'll tell you what happened out there. The White man in Baton Rouge has never had black people stand up to him like these black men stood up to them. It frightened them. When they attacked these black people and the black people did not run as they had done in the past, it scared them to death and made them back off and start shooting." What Pitcher said to explain why police didn't keep the group under surveillance over the weekend following the Friday night meeting, which he knew about, confirms the uniqueness of the Muslims' behavior: "I didn't anticipate any trouble. We've had these things before. We either talk them out or toss a little tear gas."

Pitcher secured indictments for murder and inciting to riot against fourteen men and an indictment for inciting to riot against a nineteen-year-old Southern student, Kenneth Harris. There never was a trial for murder, however. All fourteen were finally cleared of murder charges by a parish grand jury in October 1976. At that time, nine stood convicted of inciting to riot.[11]

The first trial for inciting to riot was conducted from March 6 through April 30, 1973. Before that, Warren Hall, a tenth man charged, had pled guilty and became the state's star witness. (He hanged himself in his cell in June.) The verdict was unanimous for only three; it split 11–1 for three others and 10-1 for another three. Judge Elmo Lear meted out the maximum sentence, twenty-one years, to all the defendants. Three more, including Eames, were supposed to be tried later but never were. Nor was Harris.

On April 30, 1975, the Louisiana Supreme Court overturned the convictions, ruling that Lear erred in not allowing the defense to argue pretrial for a change of venue based on a prejudicial atmosphere in Baton Rouge. On retrial the next year, the same verdicts were returned and the same sentences meted out. Then, in 1977, still another Muslim, Dudley Patrick Beavers, who had left town after the episode but was arrested in Houston in 1975, was tried. He was convicted on participating in, but not inciting, a riot and received a twenty-year sentence. The Louisiana Supreme Court threw out that conviction the following year because Judge John Covington had charged the jury improperly regarding possible verdicts. Only in March 1980 was the last trial concluded; Beavers was found guilty of participating in a riot and sentenced to twenty years.

Cumulatively, the trials were the most expensive in parish history. The heavy-handedness of the prosecutors and judges had proved as costly as the heavy-handedness of parish law enforcement.

*****

---

[1] Nick Kotz, *Judgment Days: Lyndon Baines Johnson, Martin Luther King Jr., and the laws that changed America* (Boston: Houghton Mifflin, 2005), p. 417.

[2] See Chapter 4 for its observance at LSU.

[3] The Black rallies were the culmination of a march from Bogalusa, 105 miles east of the state capital, to Baton Rouge led by Rev. A. Z. Young, president of the Bogalusa Civic and Voters League. To McKeithan's credit, he had mobilized the National Guard and state police to protect the marchers as they traveled through Livingston Parish, just east of East Baton Rouge Parish. The Klan was strong in Livingston, and it had vowed to stop the marchers. Whites turned out along the route to heckle and intimidate. In the small town of Holden, about one hundred White men gathered, and at one point, fifteen of them charged into the state police walking between them and the marchers. They were repelled, and two were arrested. The situation was also tense in Denham Springs, the largest city in the parish. Carpet tacks were strewn in the

road, and a brick and a lit cherry bomb were thrown at the marchers. After the march crossed the Amite River into East Baton Rouge Parish, Young said, "I think the protection was fine today. That place would have been a slaughter without the National Guard."

In the summer of 1965, Bogalusa civil rights activists had campaigned to force the city's White leadership to obey provisions of the 1964 Civil Rights Act, especially those ending segregation in public accommodations and employment. Their efforts were met with terrible violence, permitted and often inflicted by local law enforcement. For a short but detailed account of those events, see the paper entitled "Niggers Ain't Going to Run This Town" written in 1997-98 by Seth Hague, a history student at Loyola University in New Orleans and available online at https://www.loyno. edu/~history/journal/1997-8/Hague.html.

When times changed for the better, Young came to be regarded as one the Louisiana's great champions of racial justice. He held several positions in the administration of Gov. Edwin Edwards, including Executive Assistant for Minority Affairs. He died in 1993. A landscaped open space by the State Capitol Welcome Center is named A. Z. Young Park.

[4] Police claims that they were acting in self-defense were contradicted by the coroner's reports and, in the case of the Oliney shooting, by eyewitness accounts. Ed Price, city editor of the Morning Advocate, told me later that he had driven to the scene as soon as the police report came into the newsroom and saw the officers putting a K-9 dog back into their car. It seemed to be open season on Black youth.

[5] Police violence against Blacks was far worse in New Orleans. It occupied a lot of time by the ACLU's state office and the volunteer leadership there. Under Joseph Giarrusso and then,

beginning in 1970, under his older brother Clarence, the New Orleans Police Department was corrupt, racist and violent. Loyola University sociologist Joseph Fichter published a report in 1964 on NOPD's handling of arrestees, in which he documented routine illegal and brutal behavior. Between 1975 and 1979, NOPD officers killed more civilians per officer than any other US police force. When Ernest "Dutch" Morial was elected as the city's first Black mayor in 1978, he began to clean up the department. He dismissed Giarrusso as superintendent and brought in James Parsons, who had helped reform the department in Birmingham, Alabama, which was legendary for its racism and brutality under police chief Bull Connor. The appointment was bitterly resented by white cops, who expected the new superintendent to come from within their ranks. During Morial's tenure in office, his relationship with NOPD, especially with the Patrolmen's Association (PANO), was rocky, and his attempted reform was limited.

6   See the last section of Chapter 8.

7   One reporter was with the *Baton Rouge Morning Advocate*, the other with the Baton Rouge State-Times, both owned by Charles and Douglas Manship's Capital City Press. Douglas Manship appealed West's action, but the Fifth Circuit Court of Appeals, while agreeing that West's gag order was unconstitutional, ruled that it should have been obeyed pending appeal and refused to vacate the convictions and fines.

8   The hotel manager, Frank Fry, obviously ignorant about Black Muslims, misunderstood the name and their attire. He later told the police that he asked McKinney if they were in show business, and McKinney replied, "Sort of."

9   Two days after the fatal confrontation, Pitcher spitefully re-charged the three men for theft by fraud, a felony. That

charge was later dropped. After spending eighty-one days in parish prison, all three were released.

10 All quoted statements were drawn from an article in the *Sunday Advocate* of January 16, 1972, written by G. Michael Harmon of the Associate Press beginning on p. 18A.

11 In 1969, the Louisiana Legislature added the crime of inciting a riot to the state's criminal code (LA Rev Stat § 14:329). It was Louisiana's version of the federal act passed the year before and widely named the Rap Brown Act for the Baton Rouge native who succeeded Stokely Carmichael as chair of the Student Nonviolent Coordinating Committee, preached violent resistance, and was charged with inciting a riot in Cambridge, Maryland, in 1967. The Louisiana statute defined *riot* broadly: "A riot is a public disturbance involving an assemblage of three or more persons acting together or in concert which by tumultuous and violent conduct, or the imminent threat of tumultuous and violent conduct, results in injury or damage to persons or property or creates a clear and present danger of injury or damage to persons or property" and *inciting to riot* even more broadly, "Inciting to riot is the endeavor by any person to incite or procure any other person to create or participate in a riot." Three degrees of maximum punishment are specified, ranging from a $500 fine and six months in jail if no serious injuries or major property damage occurs to twenty-one years of hard labor if any death occurs.

# CHAPTER 10

## Moving On

Jimmy Carter wasn't my first choice for Democratic presidential nominee in 1976; Fred Harris was. A US senator from Oklahoma from 1964 through 1972, he was an economic populist and opposed the war in Vietnam. Nonetheless, when Carter won the election and assumed office, I felt I could relax. He had been strongly supported by the Black Civil Rights leadership in Georgia, and he created the Bureau of Human Rights and Humanitarian Affairs within the State Department with Patricia Derian, prominent in the ACLU of Mississippi, as its first head. He had also spoken during the campaign of ending the nuclear arms race with the Soviet Union and cutting the military budget.

At home, the civil liberties challenges had diminished in number and intensity. The ACLU motto, "Eternal vigilance is the price of liberty," is fair warning that the work is never done, but even in rural areas of the state, conditions were very different from when I joined the struggles. Organizationally, the Baton Rouge Chapter had good leaders, and the number of local attorneys

willing to take cases had expanded greatly. The state
budget continued to support both a director and a staff
attorney in New Orleans, and the volunteer leadership
was solid. I confined my involvement to the legislative
program.

In 1977, something happened that prompted me to
end my active involvement with the ACLU. For many years,
there had been an auction in New Orleans to raise money
for the state office. That year, one of the items offered was
a free abortion. The news media picked up on it and gener-
ated considerable public criticism. I told the New Orleans
leadership that they had set back ACLU's standing with
state legislators. The response was disappointing. They
couldn't acknowledge that treating so weighty a subject so
cavalierly—as if there was no difference between ending a
pregnancy and weeding a garden—was a mistake. Instead,
they wanted to cast the discussion as a debate over Right
to Choose. Frustrated, I resigned from my position as state
legislative director.[1]

In his first year, Carter's performance seemed to con-
firm my complacency about the direction the nation was
taking. His first budget included a cut in military spending,
although the cut (less than three percent) he requested was
a far cry from the "peace dividend" that we expected after
the war in Vietnam ended. And he seemed sincere about
meaningful bi-lateral negotiations over the nuclear arsenals
of the two Superpowers. By 1978, however, he was asking
for budget increases, and was sustaining development of
new and destabilizing nuclear weapons like the MX missile, cruise missiles, and Trident II, an improved subma-
rine-launched missile. Even more distressing was Carter's

commitment of US forces—personnel and weapons—to Indonesia's illegal takeover of East Timor, which Henry Kissinger had greenlighted while Ford was president but which had stalled militarily. The eventual death toll was 200,000 East Timorese. And he continued to send military aid to the repressive government of El Salvador.

That year, I reached three conclusions. One was that the forces of death controlled Washington, DC, and only a grassroots movement for nuclear disarmament, akin to the movement against the war in Vietnam, could end the arms race. Another was that it was up to me to start that movement in Louisiana. Finally, that if one is serious about justice and peace, one's commitment must be continuous and lifelong, not episodal.

So I founded the Center for Disarmament Education in 1978. Now named Bienville Center for Peace and Justice, it is still the primary organizational vehicle for peace work in Baton Rouge. An account of my participation in the successful movement to end the US–Soviet nuclear arms race lies outside the scope of this book.[2] I'll only say that it confirmed my faith in the ability of ordinary people to effect extraordinary change.

Unexpectedly, I was drawn back into a struggle to affirm civil liberties one more time before I left Louisiana in 1987 to lead a disarmament and peace organization in New Jersey. It would be misleading to say that the event entailed an act of civil disobedience on my part, because those who had me arrested were simply ignorant of their own rules. Nonetheless, I spent five nights in jail to persuade them to acknowledge their error.

It was customary for disarmament groups to leaflet at post offices on April 15 to make people aware of how large a percentage of their income taxes was spent on war and preparations for war. The War Resisters League published (and still does) a useful one-page front and back flyer that our group used every year. In 1982, a few of our members were at the main post office downtown, which had tax forms in its lobby and stayed open until midnight for last-minute filers. In the afternoon, I got a call at my office that our volunteers had been ordered off the property. So I went there and began to pass out flyers.

I knew that public facilities, with the exception of secure ones like military bases and prisons, are open to First Amendment activity as long as it doesn't interfere with the primary purpose of the facility. We were neither inside the post office nor in its parking lot but on the wide walk leading to its front door. Further, we weren't blocking ingress or egress but politely offering flyers to people as they passed. Nonetheless, in a short while, an officer with the Postal Inspection Service came out and told me I was trespassing on federal property and had to leave. My effort to explain the applicable Constitutional law to him was useless. I then told him I would leave only if I was placed under arrest. So he called city police, who cuffed me and brought me to central booking, where I was printed, mugged, and released on my own recognizance.

My trial was set for August in City Court. We waved a jury trial and let Judge L. J. Hymel decide the case. A friend, Jimmy Pearce, and Murphy Bell represented me. They made the Constitutional case, but what they hadn't done was examine the postal regulations. Had they done so, they would have been able to point out, when the postal inspector testified, that what was prohibited was commercial speech only. Hymel was unpersuaded by the First Amendment argument, ruled against me and, surprisingly, sentenced me to five days in jail. He indicated that he was certain we would appeal his ruling, so he didn't order me to start my sentence immediately.

Hymel's ruling didn't surprise me, but I found the sentence offensive. Jail time was inappropriate for the circumstances, and I knew the downtown jail was over capacity. The more I thought about it during the next few days, the more offended I became. It occurred to me that the most effective response I could make was to serve the time. I knew it would create a stir. Further, I would be out before the fall term at LSU began. After talking with my pastor, my closest friend, and my wife, I was confirmed in my decision.

My friend John Fischer said that when I went to jail, he would go to the main post office and leaflet. I told him that what he could do, when the cops came, was suggest to them that they write him a citation rather than take him into custody, an option they had in certain misdemeanor cases but which they rarely thought of using. It would spare him inconvenience and keep his prints out of the system.

On a Friday morning, I showed up at Hymel's office and told him I wanted to begin serving my sentence. He was caught off guard but agreed. John then went to the post office. The news media had been alerted and were covering both events. The postmaster, Hubert Wilfong, learned of the media presence and apparently got nervous, because he had an employee ask John to come up to his office. John had brought with him a copy of the postal regulations. He told me that he asked Wilfong to get out his copy and read with him the governing regulation. That wasn't enough to persuade Wilfong that he was in error, but he no longer felt sure of his ground. He placed a call to Memphis, the closest legal office of the postal service. Learning that staff wouldn't be in until the following Monday, he was in a quandary. John suggested that he ask city police to write John a citation and John would leave. That's how the matter stood over the weekend.

Monday, Wilfong must have been able to speak with legal staff in Memphis, from whom he learned that political speech was not included in the prohibition. On Tuesday, word came to me that Wilfong had released a public statement to that effect. Unlike the first four, I slept well during my last night in jail. Greeting me upon my release the next morning were my wife and children, friends, and TV cameras.

About a week later, I was in my office when I got a call from Wilfong. He said he would like us to come leaflet at the post office. I replied that I was sure there would be occasions to do that in the future, but we had no reason to do so now. Then as the conversation was about to end, I said, "I thought you had called to apologize."

He replied, "I was the one who got into trouble." I laughed and hung up.

---

[1]   At the time, I was not as settled in my support of reproductive freedom as I now am. Nonetheless, in public, I represented without qualification the ACLU position. Indeed, I may have been and may still be the only person to win a victory on

this issue at the Louisiana legislature, small though it was. A bill had been filed to redefine the word *person* in the state's criminal code as any human from the moment of conception. I pointed out at the committee hearing that IUDs did not prevent conception; instead, they prevented the fertilized egg from attaching to the uterine wall. I suggested to the lawmakers that they wouldn't want to criminalize every woman who used an IUD and the physicians that inserted them. Without discussion and over the objection of the lobbyist for the Catholic Archdiocese of New Orleans, the bill was amended to read "conception and implantation."

I wasn't focused enough at the time to point out how radical and unworkable such a redefinition was, imposing a burden on every pregnant woman to avoid any activity that might result in a miscarriage or a damaged infant. All of us at the hearing were just thinking of the bill as an anti-abortion initiative. Fortunately, the Louisiana Supreme Court rescued the legislature from its folly. In 1980, a Louisiana driver was charged with *three* counts of homicide because there was a man and a pregnant woman riding on a motorcycle he hit with his truck, and both people died. The court ruled that in Louisiana law murder was defined as the illegal killing of a "human being," not a "person." Further, rightly it could find no legislative intent when *person* was redefined "to broaden the murder statute...but rather an intent to legislate in the problematic field of abortion" (*State of Louisiana v. Michael T. Brown* [La., 378 So. 2nd, 918]).

2   The most comprehensive history of the global movement is Lawrence S. Wittner's three-volume study, *The Struggle Against the Bomb*. Stanford University Press, which published the volumes as they appeared from 1993 to 2003, issued Wittner's one-volume abridgement, *A Short History of the World Nuclear Disarmament Movement*, in 2009.

# About the Author

Herbert Rothschild Jr. was born and raised in New Orleans. After undergraduate work at Yale and graduate work at Harvard, he returned to Louisiana and taught in the English department and the Honors Program at LSU from 1965 through 1987. From 1990 through 2003, he worked for the University of Houston, first in Public Affairs and later in the Honors College.

Rothschild began working for civil rights and civil liberties by founding a chapter of the ACLU in Baton Rouge in 1966. He served as state president from 1970 to 1972 and state legislative director from 1973 to 1977. Among the struggles in which he was engaged were protection of free speech and assembly, reform of criminal procedure, and the rights of the mentally ill, students and women.

Increasingly concerned about the US–USSR arms race, Rothschild started the nuclear disarmament movement in Louisiana in 1978. He founded the Center for Disarmament Education, which continues as Bienville House for Peace and Justice. After retiring from LSU, he served as executive director of New Jersey SANE/Freeze (now Peace Action) from 1987 to 1990. He continued his peace work in Houston, founding the Houston Peace and Justice Center, which continues.

He also served on the board of Texans for Gun Safety from 1993 to 2001.

In 2009, Rothschild moved with his wife to southern Oregon. He chaired the board of Peace House from 2011 to 2015, serving as de facto executive director the last four years. From 2014 to 2020, he wrote a weekly column for the *Ashland Tidings*. Now he spends his time gardening, playing the flute, helping various social change organizations, and enjoying family—his wife, three children, nine grandchildren, and five great-grandchildren.